TRIALS TO TRIUMPH

TRIALS TO TRIUMPH

The Untold Story

ARTHUR "FLASH" JOHNSON

LUCIDBOOKS

Published by Lucid Books in Brenham, TX.
www.LucidBooks.net

First Printing 2011

ISBN-13: 9781935909187
ISBN-10: 1-935909-18-5

Special Sales: Most Lucid Books titles are available in special quantity discounts. Custom imprinting or excerpting can also be done to fit special needs. Contact Lucid Books at info@lucidbooks.net.

CONTENTS

PREFACE

I always felt that a fighter should come from a place of toughness.

It would be remiss if I did not say that deep down within I always felt that I would make it. I remember saying way back in high school to classmates, "If you want my autograph now it's free, but if you want it later it's gonna cost you!" I always had confidence, although for a moment in time I would lose some of that confidence, only to regain it back deeper. Despite the trials that came in my quest for success, I am happy to say I made it long before I ever realized it.

It wasn't easy growing up where I lived with a positive outlook on life, but I decided just because I was growing up in an infamously poor place, poverty and negativity didn't have to live inside of me. I believe just as we were born into sin we're also born with its attributes, like negativity, which stops many success stories from ever starting. I learned that you could be one of the greatest fighters and never go anywhere outside of your own neighborhood, or you could be an Olympian or Gold medalist in boxing and never become successful as a professional. It took me forever to realize that, but a lesson learned brings a lifetime of experience. I did not allow the negative to take precedence over the positivity, which is of God. Was His hand in my career? You bet it was. Despite the setbacks in my life, they only made for sweet comebacks.

No fighter that I have known ever enters the ring to lose, but it doesn't mean he won't. Some people say some boxing matches are rigged. If it is, only the judges and promoters are the riggers, because heavy blows can't be faked. However, I didn't write this book to give boxing another black eye—God knows it has suffered many of those without my account of it. I could never look down on it because boxing was a blessing to my family and me. My point is that if God can bless me through all I went through to achieve a lifetime goal, he can for anyone who believes. Moreover, faith begins with just one-step, no matter what others say around you or to you; your destiny can only be stopped by you.

As my amateur career ended, the standards I set have stood for years. In all 12 national titles, I was the first American amateur to do so, I was voted all American on countless occasions, I had one World challenge competition title, one Goodwill Games World title, and I was an Olympic quarterfinalist. I received some of the highest honors and achievements possible. My amateur career ended with a record of having captured approximately 170 wins and 20 losses. As a professional, my career ended with a recorded 22 wins and six losses as well as three world titles and a North American title.

To those who are young Christians today: learn to seek God very early for yourself, for in doing so you will be the better for it. I am a witness that He will lead and guide you into all truths, not just some, if you follow the desires of your heart. Even though I was a mess, confused and shackled, I had to believe that "all things are possible for those who believe" no matter how long the wait would be.

I understand now that the thing you have a desire to do most is what you should be doing.

This is the story of my life growing up in East St. Louis, my career as a world champion boxer, and my struggles as a Christian.

CHAPTER 1

My Earliest Fight:

Growing up in East St. Louis

In the city of East St. Louis, Illinois, I was received into the world by Estella N. Johnson and Arthur Allen at St. Mary's Hospital on February 16, 1966. Complications of my birth nearly cost my mother her life. Having lost a ferocious amount of blood, family members feared she would not survive the complicated birth. My oldest sister, Stella Randolph, remembers the day all too well: "We were told by doctors that at one point in time it was strictly a touch and go situation, but she pulled through. I can say that if she had died then I don't know what life would have been like without her. And I guess you could say for Arthur there was a fight to bring him into this world."

As a child, I was given the nickname "Gobble." "Gobble, Gobble," is what I would respond to, says my oldest brother, Albert Lee Johnson. "When he was just a baby crawling on the floor I would yell out to him 'Gobble! Gobble! Gobble!' and he would respond to it. Other family members started to do it as well and so it became a lasting thing. I should say we don't embarrass him these days by calling him that in public, but sometimes among ourselves we will." I guess when I was smaller I felt the embarrassment of having a nickname, but as I got older I realized the people who called me that were the ones who truly knew me. Even to this day, when I hear old friends call me "Gobble,"

I know that they know me and remember me from my earliest moments.

My family had many obstacles to overcome in order to have a decent chance at life. Opportunities for indulging in things like drugs and gang membership were all around us. The lure of these elements could really develop a person's character from a young age and we all could have given in easily. A big part of our victory came from what we were taught as youngsters from our mom. She may not have graduated high school, but she was the smartest person in the world. From her experiences, Mom knew what we were surrounded by and became a protective force for us.

Before I was born my older sister Roberta died in a horrible accident; I recall hearing lots about her from my mom, who told stories of how she died. You see, before my mother moved to East St. Louis the family lived in Little Rock Arkansas in the late 1950s and early 1960s. They had to work in the field picking cotton for a living, my mom and some of the children who were old enough then. While Mom was working out in the field on a cold day they believe Roberta, while babysitting her siblings, went to put coals in the burner and the sparks from the flames caught fire to her garment. There were different accounts of what happened that day, but Roberta was severely burned and nothing could be done to save her. I believe she died in my mother's arms and I don't believe my mom ever got over it. I suppose losing a child is something a parent can never truly get over; they just learn to move on with their life and work to make sure the other children would be protected. I think her guilt, her feeling of responsibility for this incident, made her even more sensitive to the vices that could take another of her children away.

My mother practically raised all of us as a single parent. Only later in my life would I develop a relationship with my father, who was younger than my mother, who fathered me and Regina. They never married (though he asked and was turned down by my mother) and they lived separately, but he was around enough for me to know who he was. I get the feeling that he was around more frequently when I was an infant, because I can recall things like being tossed in the air on my third birthday and I believe he was the person doing the tossing. I always felt that he favored Regina; he bought her nice things and was kind to her, but I always felt he was angry with me about something. As I grew older, I was afraid of him and began to dislike him. An example of his anger with me involved a hairbrush that he gave to me. I believe he was trying to teach me responsibility, because he told me to produce the brush every time he came over to our house. There were so many times that I couldn't find the brush, being a little kid who misplaced things easily and my mom eventually hid it from me so she could keep me from losing it. I can hardly remember a good moment with him from my childhood.

I think he tried to do what he could to take care of me and Regina. He worked at a place in East St. Louis called Shoe Court, which was one of the last businesses to leave the city. It was a popular store for shoes at that time and he always brought me and my sister new shoes. As a kid I never wondered how he got the shoes for us, I just knew that when we needed them, they were there. He cared enough about us to want to make sure we had nice shoes on our feet. One of the things my mom used to say was, "A person is always gonna notice you from the top of your head, down to your feet. Those are the first two things that people will look at when they see you." Even if I can't remember good moments with my father, I think now that this shows he tried.

I grew up with four sisters and four brothers, Stella, Pearlina, Theresa, Regina, Albert, Floyd, Calvin, and James. I am the youngest boy and my sister Regina the youngest child. There are things I can never forget from when I was growing up on Missouri Avenue. Being from a poor family, there were no summer camps or after school programs to occupy our time. We found the next best thing and that was trouble.

When I was five years old I dropped my bicycle onto my brother James' head, leaving a scar for life on his scalp (not intentionally, of course). I was trying to take my bike upstairs from the basement so that I could go outside to ride around a bit and make my own fun and I believe that James was right behind me trying to bring his bike up also. It was as if he totally ignored the warning. I remember yelling to him that I could no longer hold my bike and that I was losing my grip. I can still see in my little boy's mind that big red and white bike I had to let go of because the weight became unbearable. Boom! The bike went right smack on the top of his head and his mouth could be heard from miles away. It remains in my memory as a playful incident with my closest brother. Back in those days, it didn't seem like kids died from accidents like that, it only left a mark.

The most memorable event was a terrible accident, which involved my brother James. You would have thought he had nine lives. There used to be an old station wagon that stayed parked in the back of the duplex where we used to play. For days on end, it was never moved. James had a friend who lived next door named Benny and he and Benny decided they wanted to see what would happen if they lit a match and threw it down the station wagon's gas tank. They had nothing better to do. As they waited to see what would happen they stupidly looked down the tank and experienced a total high that they somehow lived to tell about.

The match ignited the gas that was left in the tank and it exploded in the face of James. At the time, James was the one looking down the tank, but Benny would not escape unharmed; Benny received minor burns but James received the gulp of it. After being spotted by a neighbor he was rushed inside our home were my Auntie Mae was very instrumental in helping my brother. She was able to keep him from touching his face as the ambulance pulled up to the house to take him to the hospital. That would be the last time I would see my brother for six months while he was in the hospital. My family and I can look back and we laugh about it now; kids did crazy things and somehow lived through them. Thankfully, God must have been watching over us.

During James' time in the hospital, my Auntie Mae died from a sudden illness. This was the first of many funerals I would attend. I really don't recall a whole lot on that particular day except from my little boy's eyes, seeing my mom and dad cry. I think I understood that Auntie Mae was gone, but I really couldn't process much past that. As the family walked around to view the body for a final time, someone hoisted me up to look over into the casket. *What a sweet lady*, I remembered. My mother tells a different story about how Auntie Mae would fight my grandmother (their mother). I never got a chance to personally meet my grandmother because she died before I was born. My mother told me of how Auntie Mae and she would fist fight. I thought after hearing that, *How could you ever fight your mother*? I guess I needed to have been there to understand something like that.

Auntie Mae had come to live with us because of her diabetes, which was very hard to control back in those days. I believe this is what she eventually died from. She mostly sat in our hallway, but the first time I ever saw any quick reaction from Auntie Mae was when she came to the rescue for my brother James. Her adrenaline must have kicked in quickly, because she was incredibly helpful in saving James' young life.

The lady I came to know as my Auntie Mae was old and worn. While she was alive my brother Calvin would walk on her feet as she sat in the hallway. He would just walk on her feet as if he never saw them. James, before his latest accident, would do so as well, walk right on her feet as if he never saw them. Seeing this as a kid of about five years old I thought this had to be some kind of game, because she hardly ever responded—not even an ouch or anything! Even so, often she would say, "I'm gonna get you!" but she hardly moved from her spot in the hallway. This left an impression on my young mind that it was all out of fun, so I did it a couple times, but I didn't feel good about it so I don't recall doing it very much. After the funeral I could still hear her saying, "I'm gonna get you!" I sometimes used to think about her after her she was deceased, as if she would come back and get me for walking on her feet. As I've gotten older I don't think about her much at all these days, but I do wonder why Calvin started that walking on her feet bit. There wasn't much that was funny to Calvin, but that was.

You see, my brother Calvin was born autistic. As I grew to understand what autism was, it just meant he learned things a lot slower than normal and sometimes he was not capable of learning some things at all. For a long time I thought my sister Pearlina was autistic too because I knew that she had her own struggles and I equated them with Calvin's. I found out later that Pearlina actually had ADHD and suffered from a stroke that left her with limited abilities. Because of these setbacks, she wasn't able to get a formal education; the schools that we attended just didn't know how to deal with her, so they kicked her out of school. My brother Albert remembers that Pearlina could be a violent kid, but not being able to attend school with the rest of us affected her the most. I tended to favor Calvin and Pearlina because of the struggles and learning disabilities they had, but I've learned that we'll never know why some things happen the way they do.

My brother James finally came home from the hospital and I began grade school at Cannady Elementary. Sometimes I take a ride with my family to what used to be my old neighborhood to show them where I grew up. There isn't much there at all now. The projects have all been torn down and the school, which wasn't far from there, just sits vacant with broken windows. Growing up in the projects as a kid was fun, because we made many friends and everybody just loved one another. Back in the day, your neighbor could discipline you and not get in trouble for it. Now that has all ceased to exist.

My family moved to a new location in East St. Louis called the Terran Keys projects on the north side of town. I had only ever known living on 1705 Missouri Avenue, so this was a big change for me. Even though we were moving within the projects, these buildings were much newer. In fact, the builders were still completing housing, laying walls, and pouring concrete sidewalks. I can remember when we first moved to Terran Keys, Regina got stuck inside of some cement where the builders were making a sidewalk for pedestrians. The sidewalk was just recently poured and I recall the cement came up to about her waist. Thinking back, she was trying to take a short cut to get from point A to point B. The workers handed her a shovel so that she could pull herself free. I suppose she was about four years old then and I was six, but the memory stands out to me because it was the first time I had moved and this new group of houses seemed to offer my family so many new opportunities to start over.

We may have moved to a new housing project, but the instinct we had for trouble had not left us. I was involved in an accident during my childhood that was quite serious; I was hit by a car, which easily could have taken my young life. After being disobedient to my mother, I took off to go to the store. I followed my siblings James and Pearlina and after we went to the store we decided to go to the park across from the school, I attended to swing on the swing sets. I ran across the street trying to beat an old Chevy; as a kid, the street looked forever long. I nearly made it across and right at the end, I was hit. I was blessed to have been able to walk back to where my siblings were standing, but everything appeared to be upside down! The car hit me so hard that it knocked my equilibrium off balance so that as I made it back to James and Pearlina I fell to the ground.

A lady came out of nowhere dressed in a nun's habit and immediately began to pray for me. Someone went to get my mother and later my dad showed up to fight the guy who was driving the car that hit me. People from everywhere came while the ambulance pulled up. I can still see the looks on people faces. I got to tell you the honest truth, I don't remember feeling much pain, but later on I would. After getting to the hospital I would be there for a very long time and miss about half of the school year. I remember crying out in the hospital, "I want to go home!" It took awhile for me to learn to walk and feel normal again. When I finally came back to school everyone was so glad to see I had survived and that I healed well. Being a very bright student, I was able to catch up quickly so that I would not be held back a year. Shortly after that, I continued to see doctors who assured my mother that I was totally healed of all ailments that had occurred during the accident. However, the accident left me with a minor brain injury. I would later have terrible headaches and experience blurred vision while trying to focus on simple tasks. This would last for years until God delivered me of that ailment. To this day I believe that the nun who I never knew, but who prayed for me after my accident, had a great deal to do with my recovery.

A little while later my mom decided to move out of the projects and up the street to rent a house at 1215 North 11th, it was here that I would begin to develop an appetite for boxing; at this particular time I was ten years old. My oldest siblings, Albert and Stella, had already begun to pursue adulthood and started their own families, but there were still plenty of my siblings around to make life exciting. Living at this home brought quite a few memories as well. Of course our family made friends in the new neighborhood and people from our old neighborhood would stop by because it was only about a half a mile or so up the street. However, not everyone was so friendly. In just about any neighborhood in America you have what you call "the neighborhood bully." I guess in my other neighborhoods I was too young to realize what a bully was, but just a block up the street from where we moved, lived the neighborhood bullies.

I remember a kid named Neil, a member of the bully family I would later learn, who used to come down our street and play sports with me and my brother James. Mostly we played a game of touch football. As I recall he was a very good athlete but he was also one of the most spoiled brats you would ever want to meet. At the same time Neil could be a nice kid; he once gave my mother a very nice white rug as a gift. I can't recall why. Maybe it was because he was being a generous person at the time.

Anyway while playing a game of touch football in our front yard he decided he wanted to keep my football. We were playing a silly kid's game we called "take away" in which those who were involved could not touch any of their specific belongings with both hands. Soon we decided to call timeout from that game so that we could all play touch football, but after the game was over, and because Neil's team lost, he decided to keep my ball. Neil, still claiming that we were playing "take away," said I touched the football with both hands. Everyone involved thought in the beginning that he was fooling around, but he wasn't. Neil ran home with my ball. Afterwards he was asked to bring it back, but he totally ignored everyone who asked. So we had a problem. What seemed to be a small disagreement turned serious quickly, because trying to reason with him or any member of his family was unreal. For instance, I remember them beating up an insurance rep of some sort for assuming that he was trying to cheat them out of some money and they didn't care for what he had to offer. We knew what they were capable of.

So I told my mom about the situation. She was well aware that this could be difficult because we had learned of their dealings with others in the neighborhood. But for some reason we didn't think we would have a problem with them concerning this childish matter. My mother sent my sisters Theresa and Pearlina to retrieve the ball and I don't think they felt comfortable about going to the family's house. Bam! it happened. Neil's family came out and jumped on my sisters and beat them up pretty bad over a silly ball. I suppose Neil must have told his family that my sisters were trying to take something from him that was his and obviously they believed his false report. This family was just unreal, because in their eyes Neil could do no wrong.

My mom could have let it go, but the fact that they beat up her daughters the way they did was very upsetting. She was convinced that nobody was going to treat her children that way and get away with it. Before she became a Christian, my mother was a force to be reckoned with—she was no plaything. As I recollect she decided, "I'm going to go down there to rectify this situation," so she went in her closet and pulled out a silver gun. Sometime later I learned the weapon was a .32 Snub and that she kept it hid where only she knew exactly where it was. She made sure it was loaded and started off toward their house. My brother James and I walked very far behind. As she approached their house one of Neil's relatives left to retrieve a rifle. I later learned, from one of our neighbors, that another weapon would be aimed at my mother from a distance by Neil's older brother.

You may think," *All of this because of a football?*" No, it was much deeper than that. People in this neighborhood were tired of this family. A family full of bullies was ruining the lives of those around them and my mother wouldn't stand for it any longer. This family was not at all used to being stood up to, but this day they most certainly were going to be stood up against.

As my mom knocked on the door, one of Neil's older sisters answered. I often thought, "*Where are the parents during this time?*" The sad thing was, that they were there. I don't remember seeing the father at all and so the mother would let them handle situations like these in whatever manner they pleased. In any event a conversation started with my mom.

"I would like to have my son's football back," my mother demanded.

The lady in the doorway stated, "Not until you give my brother his rug back." This was the rug that Neil gave to my mom, as I recollect.

"The white rug," my mom replied, "is no problem." But even so they were still unwilling to budge an inch on the football matter.

My mother, getting heated, then stated, "Let me tell you something, you little witch. If you don't give me my son's ball back there's gonna be some fireworks inside of your house."

As she got ready in her mind to step back and unload a round of bullets, before she could, out of nowhere came a little kid who was about two years of age. He threw the ball out to me and I made my way closer to my mom and brother to retrieve the ball. I yelled, "Mom! I got my ball!" A few extra words were exchanged between my mother and the woman at the door, but no harm was done.

Then all three of us walked home safely. As for the guy who was aiming the rifle at my mother, he would also walk away. Unknowingly, it was told to us by our surrounding neighbors, that our very own next-door neighbor had a pistol aimed at Neil's brother who had the rifle aimed at my mom from across the street during this turn of events. I suppose everyone in the neighborhood was just sick and tired of the family of bullies. I often thought about what would have happened if that kid hadn't brought that ball out to me. I wondered what prompted him to do so, or better yet, did he realize how serious of a situation was at hand at such a young age? I am convinced there was an angel among us.

Later on that day my mom made sure that they got the rug back and that would be the end of that drama. From that point on they respected our family. Sometime later I asked my mom what the last few words were about before walking home from what could have been a deadly site. She replied, "Son, I let her know I was going to put a bullet in her and she wasn't going to escape it, no matter what they were planning to do to me, she was going down." That was the very first time I saw another side of my mother. What a lady! What nerves! I also thought the same about my brother James, who was willing to go down with her, standing by her side.

I always felt that a fighter should come from a place of toughness. What kind of life would we have had if we woke up every morning and got punked? It would have been incredibly difficult for each of us, so we had to learn how to fight back. In our part of the hood, you had to be able to take care of yourself, no matter what your own issues were. My brother Calvin, suffering from autism, still had to learn to take care of himself in the ghetto.

We all knew that we had to fight. Let me tell you, I did stand up for myself, against poverty and everything that came with it.

I would continue experiencing drama like that when my older brother Floyd came to live with us after a failed marriage became whacked on a drug called "angel dust." After using it on one occasion he attempted to hurt my mother by attacking her and slamming her head against the floor in her own bedroom. As I recall, he came from the basement where he was residing at the time, into my mother's room. She was holding my sister Pearlina's baby. Floyd attacked our mother because of demons whispering in his head to do so. Fortunately there was someone there big enough to pull him off of her, my sister Theresa's boyfriend, Raydean White.

Raydean recalls, "I was a little afraid at first because of the sounds Floyd was making climbing up the stairs from the basement. I thought, What's going on? I heard noises coming from your mother's room and even though I was afraid to look, I saw him attacking her and I saw Arthur trying to pull him off of her." To this day I don't recall that part at all. It was as if I was out of my body experiencing it all. As I pulled him off of her, whatever was on him left.

After that incident my brother would be admitted to an institution for drug use. My mom was okay outside of a terrible headache from the pounding and I saw firsthand what drugs could do to anyone who used them. As my brother Floyd got better he would spend a lot of years apologizing to our mother. She would tell him, "It is alright" over and over again until he was convinced. It wasn't him that did it but the drug using that coerced him. And this same drug would cause Raydean to kill himself a few years later after marrying my sister Theresa and starting a family of their own. After seeing these examples, drugs would have no part of my life.

CHAPTER 2

The Start of a Warrior's Heart:

An Introduction To Boxing

A few years before I would ever put on a pair of boxing gloves, I experienced my first fight in school. In the third grade there was a girl name Bernice who seemed to be a pretty quiet and easygoing kid. I can't remember every detail of the fight or how it even got started, but I recall meeting her half way on the classroom floor. We looked at each other for a brief moment and I tried to make her fall by putting my leg behind her and pushing her backwards. My idea didn't work and the fight began. There were a lot of hands moving and after the dust had settled we walked back to our seats without the presence of a teacher in the room. It was as if smoke was all around me. I believe I had been dusted off by Bernice, because she was being congratulated while I was being laughed at by my peers. I saw Bernice after we grew older. She was still the same quiet person, and as we briefly spoke to one another I became convinced that I must have started that fight that took place all those years before.

My first experience with boxing came while my family was still living on the north side of East St. Louis. There was a nice man named Rallie who lived next door. Everyone in the neighborhood called him "King Cody" and indeed he was well favored by all who knew him. King Cody would issue out candy to all of the kids from the trunk of one of his many cars that he kept parked behind his house. Hershey's chocolates is what I remember. I can't even tell you how many cars were back there, for obviously he enjoyed working on them and I surmised that they were pretty old fixer uppers.

King Cody had some boxing gloves and one day he allowed some of the kids in the neighborhood to box against each other. As I walked onto the site where the boxing was taking place, I was asked if I wanted to participate. I thought mildly, *Sure, why not?* and so it was set. They very quickly found someone for me to box against; the kid's name was Eugene Johnson and I can recall it as if it were yesterday. He had a little experience in that he'd boxed before and obviously I hadn't. I heard someone say he boxed for Pop Myles, a name I would someday come to know very well. Of course after hearing the name of a legitimate gym, I became nervous. I think what made me more nervous than anything was the fact that he could perhaps knock me out. But after committing myself to put on those gloves, there was no turning back. And so we began to box.

Bang! In my face fists were flying, but I remember fighting back. Even in that moment I believe it was the start of a warrior's heart being developed from my very first experience. "No quitting!" is what I remember hearing from somewhere in the crowd. After the smoke settled I had been pounced around a bit, even so, I thought, *One day I am going to master this.*

During this time I had also begun to develop the ability to write and sing songs, so I had an imagination to someday master that as well. There I was a, little dreamer. I always believed that I was destined for greatness; a seed put there by God, which I would have to cultivate.

And so I began to envision myself as a champion from that first experience because I knew this just felt right for me. Boxing was something I feel I was put on this earth to do; even at the young age of ten, I felt boxing was my calling. Singing came in at a very close second after boxing, and of course boxing would lead to being on T.V. *Wow,* I thought, *it could happen one day.* But I knew I would have to learn the proper way to box.

My next experience with boxing didn't take place until sometime later, after my family moved to the south side of town. I must have watched a little boxing on TV, which continued to spark my interest, but I was not put into an impromptu boxing ring for a while.

My family still struggled, living in our house in East St. Louis. My sister Pearlina was involved in a dramatic situation with a guy in the neighborhood I had never seen before, a black thick young man who began an altercation with Pearlina. All I remember is that he picked up a stick and hit her. After such, Pearlina, realizing our mother wasn't home at the time, went into the closet and found that same silver gun that my mother took with her to fight the family of bullies. I suppose she watched where my mom hid the gun at some point in time, for no one else was aware of where it was. Pearlina went after that fellow to make him a ghost, but he managed to get away. She fired the .32 Snub rapidly a few times as I recall, which really scared me more than anything because she easily could have mistakenly shot one of her siblings. As I said before, there had to be angel watching over us.

My family relocated again to the south side when I was about eleven years old to a place called the John Robinson projects. We lived across the street from what was then called Lincoln High School and I attended Washington Elementary, only a few blocks away. While at Washington, I met a kid whose superstitious behavior remained with me for a long time.

He was told by his aunt, "If you talk to yourself, then you are talking to the devil."

I thought *wow, I don't want to be ever talking to him*, even though I had no spiritual understanding, it just sounded bad to be talking to the devil.

That statement made by that youngster planted a seed that began to cause me trouble because I didn't understand that it was only a saying and not a fact. It was hard for me not to talk to myself because I was a very deep thinker. So you might imagine it opened up doors for negative thoughts to really work on my young mind. I felt there was no one who I could confide in because I knew of no one at the time that had any spiritual understanding. I suffered great mind battles for some time to come as I wrestled with this issue.

But I remember a lot of fun times there at school making new friends, who to this day I sometimes see in the Metropolitan area. I remember a kid named Sammy White who used to be a high school football star and lived next-door to me. He would eventually lose his mind to drugs never to be the same again. I witnessed things like that on a continual basis, but somehow I remained unfazed by it all. Certainly my mom taught me good moral values, but in the end the decision was mine and it was in my face a lot, considering the fact that I was living in the heart of the ghettos.

It would be a year and a half later before I would encounter the opportunity to box again. Until then I could remember thinking about it on occasion, but I wasn't sure how I was going to get started. Boxing really intrigued me, but face it—coming from where I was the opportunity to box was restricted. Primarily, the chance to box would have to be nearby because I cannot remember my family ever owning any kind of transportation. My mom was very particular about allowing us to travel on our own. Since she was raising us by herself, she limited us to a certain distance from home.

And then it happened. I found out that there was a newly founded boxing gym in my very own neighborhood. Across the street from the John Robinson projects where my family lived was more housing called the John Deshield Projects. Within this neighborhood was a small center where everyone went to pay their monthly rent to the East St. Louis Housing Authority. The boxing program began here during the evening hours for all of the kids in the neighborhood who wanted to try their hope at boxing. The kids from the John Robinson projects always competed against the kids from the John Deshield projects, no matter what sport it was. I remember football games and baseball games in which we played against each other all in the name of fun, never wanting to lose to the other, each side convinced that they could beat the other.

Well boxing was no different. Having gained a little experience a year in a half earlier, I felt confident that I would be better than my first try. I hadn't learned anything since that first "match" in King Cody's yard, but I knew what it would be like to put the gloves on when most kids there hadn't even had that opportunity yet. The trainer's names were James Hooks and Benjamin Stiff, both of whom were former boxers and two guys who I would appreciate for years to come. They began working with each kid, letting us know they didn't want us trying hard to beat each other up but rather to try to develop a boxing team for the area of East St. Louis. The first team to ever be developed on the East side was the Pop Myles Boxing Club, which I would soon box against. Pop Myles was located on the north side of town and to think I never even knew it; its location was very close to where I used to live, but I guess the time wasn't right then. I probably was a touch too young and of course I certainly believe that timing is everything.

I can remember being given a form that my mom had to sign in order for me to start an amateur boxing career. But she never saw it because I signed it myself and returned it promptly. Later on I told my mother what I had done and she agreed to let me try a sport in which I was very interested, just as long as I kept up my grades in school. I played just about every sport I could as a kid, but nothing grabbed my attention like boxing. Once again I sincerely believed it was my destiny to become a boxing champion. The only thing in my life at that time that I was interested in outside of boxing was writing and singing songs.

James Hooks and Benjamin Stiff sacrificed countless hours away from their families to give an opportunity to us kids so that we could learn the sport of boxing. As former boxers they knew what it took to be good, for they had been very good amateurs and while neither ever had a professional boxing career, to speak of, they were recognized in the area for their many accomplishments. They invested their knowledge and experience into all of us who attended, with words of encouragement like, "Just make it for yourself, don't worry about trying to take everyone with you," and, "Just be the best that you can and go as far as you can go so that you and your family can have a better quality of life than you have right now." There words stayed with me, and though it would take years before I fought my way out of the projects, I did.

In these early stages of boxing I learned the basics like how to throw a jab with my left hand. As a right-handed person, I hadn't ever focused on my left hand. I found it very difficult to throw punches with my left hand, but over the course of time I learned how to use both hands the proper way. In 1979, at thirteen years of age, I embarked on what I hoped would become a successful boxing career.

During the thrill of my excitement, I was reminded that I lived in a place of hard knocks. One day while coming home from practice I witnessed something I shall never forget. A huge crowd was gathered on the playground in the John Robinson projects. Police were gathering at this time as I remember thinking, *I hope nothing has happened to Calvin, or better yet, any of my family members.* As I made my way closer to the site of the scene I saw a mother crying aloud and a policeman saying, "Take her from the scene—she does not need to see this." She had been notified of an accident involving her child. To this day I don't think she saw her child in that awful position; as I peeked through the crowd I saw a kid we all played with lying face down on the ground, dead. He had been shot in the chest by another kid we all knew, who was playing with a gun at the time. This was one of the saddest sights any human being can ever witness.

It was hard getting back to normal but we all knew we had to. Rain soon followed the accident, washing away the huge bloodstains from the playground where the death occurred. What's worse is that a couple of years later the shooter, a kid named Stymie, was killed and there was talk that the family members of the kid that died, may have had something to do with it. It was known that Stymie was found with his penis cut off and put in his mouth. That's the kind of stuff I grew up around, just brutal. I didn't think anybody deserves that kind of treatment, even though Stymie was a really rough type. There were rumors that perhaps he killed his own father and I even saw him one day while coming home from Jr. High School brutally beat up a kid to take his tennis shoes from him. Stymie was really something terrible, but he treated me nicely, maybe because he liked me for some reason or another, who knew. Even so, after having witnessed so many gruesome deaths like this, and even while participating in such a violent sport, I firmly believe no life deserves to be taken.

CHAPTER 3

"Thank God for Boxing!":
The Early Matches

In my spare time I stayed in my bedroom, shadow boxing. I imagined myself as a champion with the crowd cheering and commentators exclaiming, "Wow! What a great fighter this kid Arthur Johnson is!" I was indeed a dreamer, but I was convinced this was one dream that would come true.

One thing I've learned for sure about the sport of boxing is that guys who are supposed to be tough find out just how tough they really are. I remember that as clear as day. I'm happy to say I was never a bully of any sort. In fact, I was more of soft kid, a whiner at times. In some cases I cried about almost anything, but I had a huge heart and I knew what I wanted out of my life.

After a few months of training with some of the other kids, James and Ben thought we were ready for our first boxing contest. Of course we all were very nervous and excited, considering most of us were going out of town for the first time in our young lives. My first trip away from home was to East Moline, Illinois. Boy, it felt as though we drove forever and a day to get there. I guess there were about ten of us kids who traveled to East Moline because out of about twenty-five kids or more who tried boxing, more than half of them decided to quit before their first contest.

We experienced weighing in for the very first time. I would weigh in at seventy pounds and so would my opponent, Dwight

Johnson. His is a name in which I could never forget, because Dwight and I were the only ones to weigh in at the specific weight classification, so we would compete against each other. But what was even more special about my first boxing contest was that it was the Eastern Junior Olympics trials. The winners of each weight class would advance to the national Junior Olympics, which were to be held in the state of California that year. I thought, *Wow, if I beat this guy I am on my way! But wait a second—this is my first actual match—am I ready so soon?* I had never competed before in an actual boxing ring. We all learned how to box on a concrete floor at the center because our trainers could not afford to get a ring.

After finally being suited up for competition and stepping into the ring I was ready and so was my opponent. I was introduced as, "Arthur Johnson from T.A.C. Boxing Club of E. St. Louis, Illinois." The club name was given by James and Ben and the abbreviation stood for Thumper's Athletic Club; they thought that the name was very fitting. Across the ring was Dwight Johnson, introduced from Chicago, Illinois. After the introductions we both received applause from the gathered crowd. The bell rang and the fight began.

I remember gloves flying throughout the whole match. I fought my heart out, but Dwight would emerge as the winner. I later found out that Dwight had been to the National's to compete on another occasion and he was a bit more experienced than I was at the time. It was indeed a closely contested bout, and I loss the decision to Dwight. My trainers were encouraging after the bout, especially since it was only my first competition; they explained to me that they saw how well I had put into action our lesson and I was beginning to learn. I recall the last comments from my trainers were, "Dwight knew he was in a fight." With that being said, I felt good about the effort I gave and they assured me that I would get better.

We all loss our first bouts in East Moline, but we all fought and competed well against our opponents. Our trainers were pleased and they explained the great potential they saw in us kids. After we returned home seven more kids eventually decided they didn't want to box anymore, so the team was to be built around the four of us who decided we still wanted to compete.

Rudolph Bradley who we all called Rudy, Roderick Williams (who we called "Batman"), Cortez Dean, who joined our team after our first trip, but we would find out that he belonged, and me, Arthur Johnson (I name myself last because I feel that I had the least talent). We grew fond of each other and became the closest of friends. Rudy perhaps was the toughest, I mean even outside of the ring. But I can say he always liked me and that was a good thing because we were teammates in not only boxing but little league football as well. We once played on a team named the Metro East Flyer's for a season, which was a very popular team, even though we never won a single game. Actually, we never scored a single point. Believe it, it's true. We all spent a lot of time together over the years, working out, having fun, and getting into trouble. Rudy was very influential to me. I learned how to steal by watching him as we went to the store together.

I shall never forget the store named Coffman's, which was located right across a pathway from the projects where we lived. One day while going to the store on my own, I attempted to steal a couple packs of Kool-Aid. After being caught by the security guard my mom was quickly notified. She made her way to the store with a nice size rod in her hand and after the conversation with the store manager and the security guard, I was released into her custody. I recall being beaten all the way home with the rod she had. Today you might say that was a form of abuse, but I say it got the job done. She left an everlasting print on my mind and heart never to steal. Even though it was a very embarrassing moment in my childhood, going to jail for being a thief and a robber would have been even more embarrassing. As my mom used to say, "A thief will do anything not to get caught, even if it means taking another life," so that ability to steal had to be killed at the root and my mom felt it was her responsibility. Even though we were poor, there was to be no excuse for stealing. Proverbs states, "withhold not the rod of correction, for if thou beateth him, he shall not die." I'm not saying that's the correct way to go about rearing a child, but back in the day parents did what they felt they needed to do and we didn't call it abuse.

Soon after that incident, my mom scraped up some change to buy me that Kool-Aid I had attempted to steal. Boxing would interrupt a lot of trouble in which I could have gotten involved with. So many times, people who get into trouble are just in the wrong place at the wrong time, even though they may have been innocent. Boxing was a way to avoid these kinds of pressures because I had to stay in shape, stay committed, and remain focused on my goals. I thank God for boxing.

After my first boxing contest my second would soon follow, which took place right up the street from my home in the projects, a place called the Mary E. Brown Center. By this time more guys joined our boxing team, but they would come and eventually leave for the most part. The four of us stuck with it for years to come.

My second fight would be the only fight my mother ever came to see. I suppose she was just too nervous to watch it live. I am happy to say that I won and was convinced that I was the greatest boxer of all time, though I had a lot to learn. Still living in the projects, I clinged tighter and tighter to my vision of becoming known as a great fighter. Over the course of days, weeks, months, and years, I developed desire, discipline, and determination. I watched fighters like Muhammad Ali and Sugar Ray Leonard on T.V. and would say to myself, *I'm going to be famous one day just like they are.* I never knew the price I would have to pay.

By the time I left Washington Elementary and headed for Hughes Quinn Junior High, (another old school that's been torn down), I was into a full swing with boxing. Since I had to stay in condition for boxing by doing roadwork (another term for running), I thought that I would go out for the Jr. High cross-country team. I turned out to be pretty good because I was used to running and I was familiar with competing. That was a fun, but busy, time for me. Immediately after cross-country practice I would go straight to the gym to box. Afterwards I would finally get to go home to do home work, to eat, and to prepare for the day ahead. I had to accept the fact that if I didn't stay up on my homework I could forget about sports—my mother made sure of that.

As I grew up in the world of boxing, I started to compete more in the St. Louis metropolitan area because the team I started with had fallen apart after about two years. I remember asking why our gym had to close its doors. The people at the place where we practiced said, "We could no longer practice there because things were coming up missing and they felt we were somewhat responsible." There were other places we attempted to practice and did for a little while, but the results were the same. We needed a place of our own and so our trainers decided that we should go to another gym where we could have a secure place to work out, a place of our own.

James and Ben took us to a gym called the Pop Myles Boxing Club, a name I heard about long before I took boxing seriously. Frank Boarders was the head coach and he would take us four kids to the next level. Pop Myles had their beginnings in E. St. Louis as well, but they were now training in St. Louis, so we all headed across the river to join their team. What I recall most is that I thought Frank Boarders was one of the meanest people you'd ever want to meet. But another gentleman, James Oldenburg, who we all called Jim, seemed to be the nicest. We became close and mainly because of him I began to enjoy my stay at Pop Myles Boxing Club. James and Ben were still around to help out and show us new strategies, but little by little I grew fond of having Jim as my coach.

After joining the team and representing Pop Myles, I began to fight in more amateur bouts. I remember entering tournaments and not winning a lot because I was still learning the craft, but the more I learned, the more I won. By 1982 the Pop Myles gym moved back to E. St. Louis and boy was I thrilled. I always preferred home better and although we still competed in the St. Louis area it was good to practice on home soil. Frank Boarders and Ted Myles were able to secure the Mary E. Brown center for all of us kids to practice and to continue to learn our craft. There were fifteen or twenty kids involved during that time, and I was thrilled that Jim came along, even though he lived in St. Louis.

All of us except Frank enjoyed Jim's company and his teaching style.

You see, Jim was a white guy and most of us kids had never really known a white person. Of course we had seen a lot of white people, but we didn't know anyone personally. For me, Jim was the first white person I ever knew personally. You may wonder why I never really knew a white person, but that was because I grew up in places where white people just didn't stay. My brother James used to have a white friend named James as well, but I didn't know him personally. My brother's friend seemed to be a nice kid and I used to tell him what nerves he had because he would come around in our neighborhood to talk and play with my brother and he would be the only white kid to do so. I guess color had no limits to him; James would be out there being as black as he could be. So as I understood it, having Jim around the boxing club was unique in a good way. Frank, on the other hand, didn't care for him too much; I guess he didn't like the idea of kids looking to a white man for answers and for coaching, but because Frank knew we had come to like Jim, he would put up with having him around.

The Mary E. Brown Center was just great; it was right up the street from my home. As far as I was concerned, it couldn't have been a better place, especially since it was where I had fought my second fight. I was well into high school at Lincoln Senior High and by this time I had gained a little fame and a lot more people knew me in the neighborhood than previously. I gave myself the boxing nickname "Sugar Lope" and I used to tell people that my style of boxing was a sweet science and I could do it all from the ropes: slipping punches, throwing punches, you name it. I began to win more and gained even more attention. It was a known fact that I was never a bully of any kind in school or anywhere else and didn't get in much trouble, so for that, I was well respected.

Jim continued to make the commute over to the gym as well, teaching me things I would gladly learn because he had a way about him that made me want to pay close attention to what he was saying. Once again, Frank didn't care for that at all. I believe he felt threatened by Jim. There were times when Frank would close the gym for the day and not even tell Jim about it. I thought that was very rude, considering the fact that Jim drove from St. Louis through much traffic to get there. But Jim put up with it for as long as he could. Though I never enjoyed the way Frank Boarders taught, I think to this day he taught me about mental toughness than actual boxing skills. The bottom line is that I learned to be tough and I have Frank to thank for that.

Meanwhile, I continued to excel in academics in high school, for I worked very hard. I also had my first girlfriend, whose name was Monica. We dated a while, but nothing ever became of us. Nothing ever came of any of the girls I dated, for that matter. I believe I was too career minded for them and I knew and believed the goals I had set for myself would come true someday. The decisions I had to make didn't include having a child out of wedlock.

During the summers of 1982 and 1983 I was the only kid who showed up for boxing practice most days. No one would be there except for Frank Boarders and me, and occasionally Jim, but he was beginning to feel worn by the cold shoulder treatment from Frank.

I began to win major tournaments like the Golden Gloves year after year. Frank would say to me, "If you keep working hard, I promise you that you're going to make the 1984 Olympic Team." I wasn't sure if I could since I hadn't gained as much attention nationally as I had locally, but in time I did. All that work and dedication started to show. By this time Rudolph, Roderick, and Cortez all began to fade away from the world of boxing, but we still remained friends. Later, Rudolph would enter the Army and continued to pursue boxing there. Roderick and Cortez often came in and out of the gym, but they were never fully persuaded to continue to box seriously. Those guys were at one time all better than me, but my heart would not allow me to throw in the towel, no matter how difficult it got. I had tasted success and I wanted more.

CHAPTER 4

Nationally Known:

Light Fly Division National Champion

I remember entering my first national tour in Kansas City, Missouri in 1983 and fighting a kid named Terry Dominique. This kid was very strong. I fought in the 106 pounds weight class, the light flyweight division, but I only weighed 98 pounds. At seventeen years old I was considered an open boxer, which is the last classification of division an amateur boxer competes in before fighting professionally. I had boxed in every other division and now entered in the light flyweight class. I felt that I would surely grow into the division without a problem, but 106 pounds was the lightest weight class for an open fighter and I wasn't quite there yet. Even though he weighed much more than me, I was set to fight Terry for my first national match. I must tell you that this kid hit me harder than I had ever been hit in my entire life. I felt pain from the top of my hair strings to the bottom of my feet. Even though he hurt me I fought back harder, but still, Terry won a unanimous decision over me.

It didn't hurt so bad to lose there because that was my first time at a national tournament and I knew that to get to Kansas City meant I beat out the kids in Springfield Illinois and won the Golden Gloves. So I chalked it up as experience. Outside of losing I had a great time. I remember hanging out with another member of the Springfield National Golden Gloves team, named L.C. Robinson. I mention him because he was responsible for taking me into a restaurant and allowing me to eat as much as I wanted and convincing me to leave without paying. He told me to go wait outside while he paid at the cash register for our meals. So as I waited he walked up to the cashier and turned the other way and ran, yelling to me, "Run! Don't let them catch you!" As an idiot, I ran. We didn't get caught, but if we had, we would have been in some deep trouble. I made sure not to tell that story to anyone when I got back home.

After getting home and resuming my training schedule I earned more opportunities to enter National tournaments by beating out the kids in my area once more. I boxed in the Amateur Boxing Federation and the Ohio State Fair National Boxing Tournament and eventually I began to win more of these bouts. I started to gain attention across the country and my confidence was boosted. I persevered whether I was winning or losing.

I entered the Western Olympic Trials with a desire to represent the United States on the 1984 Olympic Team. However, tragedy struck my family again and almost ruined my opportunity. My sister Pearlina married a man named Henry Lee Walton, whom I grew to love. He became very ill and I remember going to the hospital to see him before I left for trials in Colorado Springs. Right before the competition I was notified by my family that Henry died. A new friend and member of the St. Louis boxing team I was now a part of, Michael Cross, was also competing in the trials as a middleweight. Michael helped me to get through the situation so that I could compete. Although he came up short in his bid to win the middleweight division tournament, he recalls the competition well: "Arthur [was] very shaken by the death of his brother in law and I would try to comfort him as best I could. I guessed I did because he went out and did his thing. He put it on those little dudes."

My first step was to beat a kid name Johnny Tapia. Among others I would face in the tournament, Johnny had beaten me earlier in 1984 on a very controversial decision, but in the Olympic trials I won convincingly. Beating Tapia bought me a ticket to the Final Olympic Trials in Fort Worth, Texas, where other athletes such as Evander Holyfield and Mike Tyson competed to try and make the 1984 Olympic team. My bid for the team was not successful, as I lost to Michael Black in the quarterfinals of the Trials. Even though I lost that year, it would only serve to make me more determined to be the best and one day make the Olympic team.

Johnny Tapia would go on to become a professional boxing world champion, as well as others I defeated in the amateurs like Eddie Cook, Michael Carbajah, Kennedy McKinney, David Grimman, and Terron Millet. Wow, to think that all these guys I beat would someday be champions of the world would have been quite hard for me to imagine in those days.

Though I didn't go to the Olympics, the fall of 1984 served me well; I won another major national title. This one was a really big deal to me because I was seen all over the world by sports fans for the first time, by those who knew me and those who didn't. ESPN brought my television debut to the millions who watched. This tournament featured a man named Mike Tyson as the heavyweight champion. Mike and I became pretty good friends during this time. He had a habit calling me "AJ" over and over again, to the point that I asked him once if he was crazy (to that he didn't respond). After watching me, Mike would say, "I want to knock my opponents out like you." The whole thing was surreal because by this time I had created a bit of attention for my boxing ability.

What's so amazing is that I can remember this as if it was yesterday. I remember the names and faces of the guys that I fought against. I can remember thinking, *I finally got to be on television and all my neighbors and friends saw it happen*! This particular tournament I won was called the Junior National, the winners of which would go on to the Jr. World competition. Before we competed across the world, it began in Lake Placid, New York. I was still in the light flyweight division and I remember beating Cecil Thompson, who turned out to be a pretty good professional fighter. In the finals of the tournament I beat Fernando Gonzales, which was seen on television.

Returning home was great. For the most part everyone had seen the fight and I had become a local hero as well as a national figure. There wasn't anyone from the city of E. St. Louis to ever reach the heights I reached in boxing. But I kept my head on and enrolled in college to pursue my education in broadcast journalism. My mom was good at directing me in that area. She would tell me, "There's nothing that's a for sure thing in life," and I would find that out later for myself. I believe that my mom was one of the smartest people I've ever known, even though she never made it passed the third grade in school. To me, that's the most remarkable thing. I'm sure she would have loved to have had more education, but circumstances didn't allow it. Working in the cotton fields in Little Rock was very demanding, but wasn't nearly as tough as raising nine children in East St. Louis as a single parent.

Time was approaching for me to compete Internationally as part of the Junior World competition. The team had been formed by the winners in Lake Placid, who would now compete in Europe. Although Mike Tyson won in Lake Placid, he elected not to compete in Europe, but decided to turn pro instead. He would later become the youngest heavyweight champion of all time. Competing in the Junior World competition meant it would be my first opportunity to travel out of the United States. I marveled at the site of the Big Ben in London and various other sites I enjoyed. While I was in Europe, eating brunch one day with the team, an elderly man apart of the European boxing organization approached and gave a prayer and cried afterwards, perhaps because it was a moment in time he really appreciated being a part of. For some reason that particularly touched me and I've never forgotten that.

As far as the competition was concerned, the outcome there would be no different than Lake Placid. I knocked out one opponent and easily defeated another to become the 1984 Junior World competition champion in the light flyweight division. This championship title would set the stage for years to follow. After competing I was chosen as the most outstanding boxer of the competition and took a pose to have my picture taken with legendary former fighter Henry Cooper.

By 1985 I was a dominant figure in amateur boxing, winning national tournaments and being selected on many occasions as the most outstanding boxer in the country. That was a huge moment in the sun, for I had achieved something that no other amateur boxer in the United States ever had; I won several National titles in quick succession. Everything I dreamed was happening.

When 1986 rolled around I experienced a life changing moment. By this time I had exceeded the expectations of all the former boxers from the city of East St. Louis, Illinois and St. Louis, Missouri. The tension between my trainers, Frank and Jim escalated to an all time high. I recall one day while Jim was showing me how to throw a left hook out of nowhere Frank began to yell at Jim, "That's not the correct way you're showing him to throw that punch!" Jim, as his manner was, took it all in mildly and didn't say much, but later on he decided he'd had enough of Frank disrespecting him. Frank was tough; as I recall it was his way or no way at all. I struggled with Frank's style and Jim would later call me on the phone to say he wasn't going to be involved with the Pop Myles gym any longer. I was devastated.

I would see Pop Myles many times when I did roadwork in the mornings at Lincoln Park, which was where the Mary E.

Brown Center was located. He would be there working with other kids who enjoyed swimming and other sports that were available to kids at that time in the community. My main two coaches were not getting along and James and Ben weren't around anymore after giving me my start in boxing, so I decided to leave the Pop Myles gym as well, to go and begin training at other gyms. One of the gyms I attended was called Twelfth and Park Recreational Center in St. Louis, where Leon and Michael Spinks got their start in boxing and with the same trainer, Kenny

Loehr. The time I spent there was most enjoyable because I was able to continue to enhance my knowledge of the sport. Later I would spend my most memorable moments at a gym called Cochran Recreational Center. Jim came along to assist me as my coach, even though Cochran already had their own coach named Winston Shaw. I also thought he was one of the nicest person I had met; Winston had no problem allowing Jim to come and train me, considering most trainers who head a gym always like to be recognized as the head honcho, but Winston was different in that aspect. Even to this day I sometimes think about that gym because as time would allow it, the Cochran gym would be a part of my life for many years to come.

CHAPTER 5

Setbacks Create Comebacks:
The Goodwill Games

In my first Senior World Championship in Las Vegas, Nevada, I lost to an international fighter from Turkey. The loss hurt me, but only for a moment because I felt sure that I did enough to win that particular bout. I was beginning to find out that politics ruled the world of boxing. Although the World Championships were held in the United States, the foreign judges sided with the foreign fighters. My efforts would have proved to be enough for a U.S. win, but I believe a statement was being made to the U.S. team: although the World Championships were on our home soil, there would be no favoritism at all displayed to the U.S. fighters. The officials seemed not to consider the fact that everyone competing had to win preliminary bouts to get that far to represent their country, so obviously we were good enough, no matter which country we were from. I took it as I had to and went home a bit disappointed.

I was still living in the projects at this time, but getting closer to moving out to a higher standard of living. The loss in Las Vegas left me with the feeling of being knocked backed a step from my goals. A week after I had arrived back home, Jim called and asked me what my plans were. I told him that I was going to rest awhile and decide later on what I would do. He replied, "This is not the time to stop and rest awhile, but to pick yourself up and let the boxing world know that you are still the best."

I took his advice and became well selected as an All-American and the U.S. asked me to represent our country in the very first Goodwill Games to be held in Moscow, Russia. A team of twenty four boxers were chosen, two in each of the twelve weight classes, which started at the light fly division, weighing in at 106 pounds, all the way up to the super heavy weight division which was 201 + pounds. This time I was a flyweight, weighing in at 112 pounds since the championship fight in Las Vegas. A camp was formed for the boxers in Colorado Springs, where we spent many weeks in preparation for the games in Russia. All the while Jim encouraged me to become even more determined to prove that I was not only the best in the U.S., but the best in the world. My confidence was now at an all time high, doubled by my newfound faith in myself.

Going to Russia would be one of the greatest experiences of my life. I can remember asking, "Why doesn't it get dark until 10:00 pm?" I thought that was very unusual, and one of the greeters replied," that the countrymen enjoy setting the times so that it stays daylight for as long as possible. Interesting, upon arrival we were each given translators; the translator that was assigned to me told me that I was her favorite of all the boxers, maybe because of my quietness and respectfulness toward others. The majority of the guys who were there were everything but respectful and I recall guys getting into trouble and so forth. I recognized even then that I have my mom to thank for rearing me up right. She would say things to me like, "If you get in trouble there will always be a place for you to be put," and "a hard head will make you have a soft behind." Those words I never forgot because they reminded me of where I came from and the repercussions of my actions. As the tournament began I took down all of my opponents in convincing fashion, defeating a very experienced Hungarian who was a bronze medal winner in the 1980 Olympics (which the U.S boycotted). Among others I beat a Brazilian, a Venezuelan, and a Russian in the finals to win the gold medal in the Goodwill Games. This is also where I earned the nickname Arthur "Flash" Johnson from the sports broadcaster. One of the commentators for this event was Football Hall of Famer legend Paul Horney.

My victory left no doubt that I was the best in the world at this weight division. Out of all the boxers from around the world who participated in the Goodwill Games, I was chosen as the outstanding boxer of the competition and, amazingly enough, I was the only non-Soviet to win a gold medal in the boxing competition. The Soviets won 11 out of the 12 weight classes. I considered this to be my highest achievement yet. And to think, if I hadn't lost in the World Championship in Las Vegas, I wouldn't have been able to participate in the Goodwill Games. As fate would have it, losing equaled an opportunity for winning. There is a reason why certain things take place in life, for my newfound faith made me aware that all things work together for the good of those who love God and trust in him.

After I returned home from Russia the city of East St. Louis rolled out the red carpet for me. A celebration took place with a parade and among other festivities; I received a plaque from then Mayor Carl E. Officer. I also received a telephone call from then Heavyweight Champion of the world, Larry Holmes, who congratulated me on my accomplishment.

Across the river, the city of St. Louis also recognized me for my accomplishments. I was invited to Busch Stadium to throw out the first pitch before a Cardinal baseball game. After the game,

Hall of Famer Ozzie Smith gave me the ball with which he made the last catch and the Cardinals won the game.

I was also invited to attend the Kronk boxing stable were I met the legendary Hall of Fame trainer, Emmanuel Steward, which is where Hall of Fame boxer Thomas Hearns trained. Emmanuel and I talked about future decisions concerning the offers I had to turn professional. I ultimately decided to hold out to weigh my options, because I never wanted any decision I had to make to be guided by a dollar.

After everything cooled down a bit the City Hall Office and Mayor Officer made a promise to support me in accomplishing my continuing pursuit of a gold medal in the upcoming 1988 Olympics. They reneged on those words; I remained living in the projects because as an amateur boxer I could not receive money for participating in competitions. However, I imagine that if my skin color would not have been black that would not have been the case. I've never been one to use the race card, but this was obvious. Everybody and their mother knew who I was at this time, but as I was taught, I kept pressing on because I knew that the projects was only a place I lived and not equal to my promising future.

I enrolled once again into college at Southern Illinois University in Edwardsville, Illinois to continue my quest for an education. I had taken a small break from school because my schedule became very demanding and I had to be focused on boxing, but I never forgot that my mom said, "Nothing is a for sure thing in life."

After my impressive showing at the Goodwill Games it was clear that I was the man to beat. I knew I still had to work harder and not take my opponents for granted. Looking back I guess at this point that I was indeed on top of the world, but even so, I would still make time for socializing with my friends. Cortez and I remained great friends. We even got together to share our talents and sing. Cortez began to make plans for us to sing at local churches—he was like a miniature agent, booking the two of us anywhere he could. People would see us and say, "Isn't that the guy who's the boxer?" But all the more I enjoyed it, the songs were great, people enjoyed hearing us sing, and we were always given a great deal of compliments after we were finished performing. It felt as though I was bringing to life the second part of my childhood dreams by singing and writing music.

CHAPTER 6

A Need for Something Greater

In the midst of all of my great accomplishments, something was missing from my confidence. I had questions that needed to be answered. I wasn't directed by outside influences, like drugs or alcohol, but regardless of that, I needed a savior to fill the void I grew to recognize in my life.

Years before I decided to live as a Christian I saw my mother live the life like no one I ever knew. I mean, my mother used to be a force to be reckoned with until she accepted Christ into her life. She was not a bad person by any means, but it was no secret that she wasn't a saint either. I saw a 180 degree turn in someone's life because of Jesus and I thought, *It can't be all bad*. So I saw a need for Jesus to become a part of my life. I did not know that as I grew to know Him that He would be the major source of my life.

I've managed to pick up a saying, "What you do speaks so loud I can't understand what you're saying," but this was not the case with my mother. Everybody who once acquainted themselves with her knew she exemplified what a Christian life should be like. This lady would hug the cashier at the grocery store, she just had so much love to give. Hearing her pray, watching her go to church was as good of a witness I could have ever seen with human eyes.

I was tortured for years by a child's idea that if I talked to myself, it meant I was talking to the devil. For years I could not help but to talk to myself because I had no savior to help ward off the attacks of the negative thoughts that came. It was as if there was a constant war inside of me. Because I was a very serious person, I took things to heart that I shouldn't have—silly things, like when someone said to me as a kid that when a person points at you that means your mother is going to die. I must have been about 11 years old when I heard that and I really took it to heart. I now realize as I look back that it was crazy for me to believe in these superstitions, but that's the way it all went down for me; I was an impressionable and serious kid. By the time the adversary, who I now know as the devil, was done torturing my mind, I was left with what I now know was likely some form of schizophrenia, which is when you hear voices in your head all the time. Through all of my achievements, this was my own personal secret. I was ashamed to ask for help and I remember crying out loud because it was just unbearable.

To this day I am so very thankful my mother made me go to church with her, because I learned that no matter what I accomplished in my life, there would be a void if Christ did not live in my heart. So as I often witnessed my mother's life, I began to really notice my life and understood that I didn't personally know who Jesus really was. My mother was a great Christian example for me and so was another lady named Clara Johnson, who had witnessed to my mother before she became a Christian. I began to talk to them both about accepting God in my life, but I had one major question: Would I have to stop boxing?

Clara had a lot of wisdom and her response was, "Let God direct your pathway. If He doesn't want you to fight anymore, He will let you know. He wants what's best for you."

Since I was having this war within myself anyway, I felt that I should trust Him to see if He really cared enough to help me. But I also worried, *What if he doesn't want me to fight anymore? What will I do?* Since I had invested so much time and energy to become the best I could be and I was finally at the top of my game, I felt if He wanted to take it from me, then who needs Him?

But through Clara's comforting words, I found peace when she said to me, "God is not into hurting people, as many may think. For if He takes it from you, He will give you something better in return."

But still I halted at the thought because I enjoyed doing what I had become very good at doing, but Clara continued to support by, saying, "Don't worry. God isn't concerned about taking anything you aren't willing to give up. He will guide you along the way."

I felt better and willing to accept Him as my personal savior at this point in my life. Before this conversation with Clara, I was used to hearing Christians say what they could not do and I was not interested in getting involved with something that would make me feel even more sorrowful than I already felt inside. Why would I want to place more restrictions on my already impoverished life? Why would I want to join a group of people whose only concern was about what they cannot do?

But, after accepting Christ, I learned that I could do all things through Christ who strengthens me. On January the 15th 1986, I received the baptism of the Holy Spirit and began to speak with new tongues as the spirit of God gave me the utterance. I was new. My old life had passed away; instantly the secret war in my mind was over. God had set me free, and I mean totally free. Amen!

After my spiritual new birth friends saw the new me. They thought I was pretty weird because when I first became a Christian I would often say, "Praise the Lord!" They would say, "He's flown over the cuckoo's nest. How could this happen to such a great athlete?" If they only knew the war I had before accepting God, they would have said, "Praise the Lord!" with me.

In time they saw that it didn't affect my ability to box and they accepted my new life. I became comfortable as a witness before them and my friend Cortez Dean who accepted Christ a couple of months later. As we maintained our friendship through the years after we started boxing together, I suppose he saw something in me that caused him to go after God, and for that I'm glad.

I kept my schedule busy with boxing, but I still found time to enjoy the things I liked doing, like singing gospel songs at churches with Cortez. He booked us to sing at any church that would allow us, and one day in the fall of 1986, Cortez had signed us up to sing at a local church I had never been to. I remember this particular church reminded me of "The Little House on the Prairie" with its form and a look of quaintness amidst East St. Louis. There was a young lady there whom I never even noticed, but as we sang our songs during the church program, I became the apple of someone's eye.

As the service dismissed and Cortez and I began to walk towards his vehicle, a young lady grabbed my attention by saying, "Hi, my name is LaTanya. You may have heard that somebody at this church likes you and it's me."

Cortez found out through another friend of his that a woman had spotted me at another church service singing, so I had been somewhat warned that a woman was interested in meeting me. Still she caught me by surprise. Bam! Just like that, she took my breath away with her courage. What a bold thing to do, to approach someone she'd never met before and say, "I like you."

As she introduced herself, my head dropped. I hadn't seen her and to be honest, I was afraid of what she might look like. With my head still down, I replied, "Okay," and she asked for my telephone number. I thought, *Sure why not?* I couldn't look at her, even once, because I didn't think I would have the nerves to say no. I just wasn't a bold kind of a person. I thought, *What have I've gotten myself into?* or better yet, *What has Cortez gotten me into?*

I found myself looking forward to receiving her phone call, and when she finally called about a week later I asked, "What took you so long to call?" I was very curious about getting to know this person I met only a week earlier, but whom I didn't necessarily see with my eyes. As we talked on the phone, getting to know each other a little bit better, I never admitted to her that I really hadn't seen her face.

On the phone I learned that this young lady didn't know anything about me or my accomplishments and that felt different, but good to know that she had goo-goo eyes for me for who I was and not because of what I had become. During one of our many conversations she revealed to me that she had a child who was only three months old. I knew that my rebuttal could change everything in terms of our future relationship,

My response was simple: "And … so what else do you want to tell me? You used to be a man and now you're a woman?"

She replied, "No," and I chuckled a little. I could tell she had been through a disappointing relationship beforehand and she was thankful that no wedding vows had taken place. I felt, *Who was I to hold anything against her or to be judgmental towards the situation?* She had already received enough criticism without my assistance and she would later explain to me that she felt that the biological father was the wrong person to have fathered her child. It would take a long time for her to experience healing because of this past relationship. Obviously there were issues that had to be dealt with, but I assured her that she and I could have some type of relationship, even if we turned out to be just friends. I had a feeling she wanted more than my friendship and that was something I wasn't willing to give in to at this time. Before meeting LaTanya I had been dating someone else, so a relationship with her didn't seem to be in the near future. As more time elapsed we arranged for our second meeting; LaTanya invited me over to her house to cook dinner for me.

I climbed out of my mother's car and approached LaTanya's front door. Fancy dressed as I was in my black and white suit, I thought that the worst thing that could happen is that we would only become friends. I was nervous, because, as I mentioned, I never fully saw her face. I did however, take a small glance before dropping my head down in our prior meeting and I remember seeing some big Harry Carrey glasses on her face. The thought of those glasses ran sharply through my mind as I knocked on LaTanya's door.

The door opened and I was asked to come in. As I made my way into her home, I looked for LaTanya to come around from another area of the home to greet me, but to my surprise it was her that opened the door. I didn't recognize her without the glasses and her hair was combed softly back. I immediately thought, *This is a nice looking black woman.*

She invited me into the kitchen where she had prepared a meal for me and we talked. The more I looked at her the more I thought to myself, *This woman is very good looking!* Dinner was great, although LaTanya didn't eat because she had a bite before I arrived and so she watched me eat and I had no problem with that. That was the beginning of a long lasting relationship. I would later meet her child and instantly fall in love with her. Her baby girl's name was Lakeisha. Shortly after meeting Lakeisha I was allowed to take her home to meet my family without the presence of LaTanya. She had a few errands to run, but she would show up a couple of hours later. I was surprised that she would trust me so openly, so soon, with her child. I guessed she must have really felt comfortable with me and I wasn't about to disappoint her. When LaTanya arrived she met my family and played a game of touch football with me. I guess having all brothers certainly helped because she could actually play and was pretty good at it. She was something!

I found out later that she enjoyed sewing, so I asked her to make me a couple of boxing uniforms. She agreed and took my sizes and hooked me up. She had three brothers who were well aware of who I was and they would proudly inform her when she got home. Even though I had asked her to make me a couple of boxing uniforms she did so without questions and did not connect my request with my local fame at that time. Then one day it happened; LaTanya saw me on television and later exclaimed, "I didn't know you were a boxer!"

LaTanya showed herself to be a dear friend to me. After meeting her family we kept in touch more often, but even though she was a very pretty young lady, I wasn't thinking about a serious relationship. I was so focused on my childhood dream of making it big someday that I didn't want anything to stop that.

CHAPTER 7

Fighting for Gold:
The 1988 Summer Olympic Games

By 1987 I was virtually unbeatable in the United States, going three years without a defeat to an American. I continued to compete and win again and again, setting standards that stand-alone even to this day. I represented the United States in all the major championship competitions and still had my eye on competing in the upcoming Olympics.

Yet in the midst of my accomplishments, I suffered having my hands broken several times. I was given cortisone shots to relieve the pain in my hands so I could compete. The shots were administered by the doctors of the United States Olympic Committee and I was incredibly careful about what I put into my body.

The first injury happened at Abercrombie's training camp in Houston, Texas. I liked this camp because I was invited to spar against boxers like Orlando Cannizalas and Calvin Groove, both of whom went on to be professional world champions. Abercrombie's training camp had an interesting back story; the Misses was a widower and happened to be the third richest lady in the world at this particular time. For some reason, Mrs. Abercrombie wanted to invest money into boxers that she felt had a chance of becoming champions someday. Her camp was run by a gentleman name Bob Spagnola, who was a very decent human being. I guess I never understood why this woman was willing to spend her money on a training camp for boxers, but I have always been thankful for people like her.

1987 continued to go exceptionally well, although I would finally lose to an American later in the year. However, I came back to beat that same opponent twice a few weeks later, proving the loss was only a fluke. His name was Jesus Arreola and he would be the last American to ever beat me during my amateur career.

The greatest thing that happened that year was that I moved out of the projects. I had become discouraged about the fact that I was the best in the world, but I still lived in the hood. One day while talking to my brother James about the matter, he said to me, "Gobble, there's a lot of your friends that are going into the armed services to get out of the projects, but you are going to fight your way out these damned projects." And I would.

I told my mother that I would never need public assistance again, because for years I had experienced the use of food stamps and other things that we had to use to get by because we were poor. It wasn't a put down to my mom, because she did the very best that she could under the circumstances. It was just that I didn't want that type of life for *my* future. My mom understood that, but she had a lot of wisdom, as she would reply, "Son, never say what you won't do." I had to learn that later, for myself.

Because I was at the top of my game, I finally met the people who were willing to help me move forward in life. A gentleman by the name of Merle Taylor was pretty big in the boxing program in St. Louis and he had heard that I was interested in moving to Minneapolis, Minnesota. I had taken a trip there to see my sister Theresa, who had relocated there, and I was ready to try something different. After visiting with my mom, we both decided it was time to make a change. One of the largest contributing factors was the city of East St. Louis itself. The city was very negligent in leaving the flood gates open during a normal rainstorm earlier that year, causing millions of dollars worth of damage to many people's homes in the area, including my family. The area in which we lived suffered most profoundly. It would be years later before the city would have to pay retribution for the great lost.

After all of this, we were ready for a change. Merle contacted me and put me in touch with a man name Bill Jaffa, who lived in Minneapolis and would become my new boxing coach. Bill turned out to be very instrumental in helping my family to relocate to Minneapolis. While I was ready for the move, saying goodbye to friends was not easy; Jim and I would continue to keep in touch from time to time across the distance, but Cortez decided he wanted to come along. Cortez lived with my family and me until he could get a place of his own. The hardest goodbye of all was the one I made to LaTanya. I can still recall tears rolling down her cheeks. I made a promise to keep in touch with her, and I did.

I continued my training in Minneapolis until the time came for me to compete in the trials for the 1988 Olympics. Coming off of my hand surgery I had to beat the then National Golden Gloves Champion who became champion in my absence. I won in a decision and took down 2 other highly ranked opponents, proving my dominance and ensuring my spot on the 1988 Olympic team.

Trauma surfaced by the end of the year. My mom got breast cancer, a fight in which my entire family would become a part of. Although I had surgery on my right hand earlier in the year, this was no comparison to what my mom was up against. Her illness would take precedence over everything that I was doing at the time, for I was very concerned about her situation. Everything seemed to be going smooth with the relocation to Minneapolis, except my mom's battle did not go as well as the family had hoped. She would have to have surgery, but the surgery alone did not cure the problem because there were some areas the doctors did not detect in time to remove. My mother went through chemotherapy treatment, which allowed her to go into remission for a great while.

LaTanya and I stayed in touch, taking trips in between competitions to see her. During this time, right after I found out I would represent our country in the 1988 Olympic Games, I realized that I was deeply in love with her. I asked her to be my wife and she said yes.

Just before going off to training camp to prepare for the Olympics, LaTanya and I were married. The wedding took place in the backyard of LaTanya's family's home with both our families and friends in attendance. Cortez was the best man, baby girl Lakeisha was the flower girl, and my wife's best friend Lisa Merritt was her maid of honor. I sang a song I wrote, titled "Make You Mine," before we said our wedding vows to one another. Originally, we had planned the wedding for December of that year, but upon my request, before going off to Seoul, Korea to participate in the Olympic Games, LaTanya agreed to marry me then. I adopted Lakeisha immediately.

GAMES OF THE XXIVᴛʜ OLYMPIAD

1988 U.S. OLYMPIC BOXING TEAM

Making the Olympic Team was a dream come true for me. I couldn't have imagined that this would happen the very first day I put on a pair of boxing gloves and boxed against a kid name Eugene Johnson. It seemed ages ago. Wherever this kid was, I am sure he had heard about my success and perhaps told his friends, "I beat him up a long time ago." He's right, he did.

I was still determined to go all the way to capture another gold medal. I was on the 1988 Olympic team with guys who would go on later to win professional world titles, such as Riddick Bowe, Ray Mercer, Michael Carbajah, Kennedy McKinney, and one of the most popular of all, Roy Jones Jr. It was great being at camp with all these guys. We trained together for about three months at various sites like Fort Huachuca in Arizona and the Olympic training center in Colorado Springs, Colorado. I spent so many days in Colorado that it was like a second home after a while. Before we went to Seoul our team had a match against Canada and we defeated them pretty bad. After this, my Canadian opponent would not attend the games, even though he won the right to represent his country, because of his defeat in a fight against me. I was pretty dominate throughout the bout with him and his trainers felt that perhaps he wasn't ready for the high caliber competition that he would find at the Olympics. I felt that was an injustice to him. I certainly didn't think that was a reason for him not to be able to show his talent to the rest of the world and represent his home.

After each international bout we swapped jerseys with the other team; it was something to remind us athletes of the countries we competed against. After the dual with the Canadian team, we resumed our training. During our camp Hall of Fame boxer Sugar Ray Leonard offered training tips while working out with us in preparation for the Olympics. Before leaving for the 1988 Olympic Games at Seoul Korea we stopped off in California to have a big celebration at Disney World before leaving the country.

I can remember the anticipation as well as the flight stopping in other countries like Germany and Japan before landing in Seoul. It was now time for me to go for the gold. I was the first to compete from the United States boxing team in the Olympics. There was only one guy per weight class, so only twelve boxers made the team, unlike the Goodwill Games in which the U.S could take two in each weight class, and unlike track and field where multiple athletes can represent a country. In most cases boxing is totally an individual effort; every man had to be for himself. Even though we were on a team and wanted to see the other guys do well, it was still personal. As I opened up for the team, my first win brought great hope for a U.S Gold medal.

My first two wins landed me in the quarterfinals at the Olympic Games where I had a new challenge. Throughout the Games, I fought with an injured hand, as I had during the trials competitions. My hand never healed well enough for me to be a hundred percent, but I am not one to look for excuses.

I was up against Seoul's favored World Championship winner. In 1986, Kwang-Sun Kim fought to win the world title in Las Vegas, so I knew this was going to be a tough fight. The match between Kwang-Sun Kim and myself was one of the most exciting bouts of the Olympics. As the fight took place dignitaries, including the Korean president, found their way in to witness our bout. In the end, Kwang-Sun Kim won in a controversial decision.

I took the defeat hard. If I had known what I know now, I would have enjoyed my stay instead of allowing the loss to make me deeply depressed. Quite frankly, not many people ever get the opportunity to realize their childhood dreams, so I needed to look on the bright side of things. I made it onto the U.S. Olympic Team and I traveled to Seoul, Korea to fight against the best boxers in the world. Statistically less than one percent of those who shoot for things like the Olympic Games actually make it, so with that in mind, I did my best to be happy.

My wife, LaTanya, made the trip over to cheer me on and to console me in my disappointment. She was the best cheerleader anyone could have asked for. I placed fourth and did not receive the medal I had hoped for, but I remembered the words of my mother: "Nothing's a for sure thing." Two years earlier, I won the gold in Moscow, but this gold would belong to Kwang-Sun Kim. I had to accept this.

Interestingly, we found out later that the judging of the Seoul Olympics was rigged. In other words, the changing of money took place for judges who scored in favor of Korean boxers. The Koreans would be excluded from the 1992 Olympics.

After the Games were over we headed back to the U.S. LaTanya and I stopped off in California to visit my brother Albert before going home to Minneapolis. Albert watched me box on television and was excited to see me. We left California and headed home, where I received many awards and much applause. I was inducted into the Minnesota's Wall of Fame with many dignitaries, including the governor, being present. After my return, I was also invited to the White House in Washington D.C. to meet President Ronald Regan.

I look back at the time that followed the Olympics and I realize that I learned that success is not made of what a man has, but what the man is made of. After all, to achieve something you have never before accomplished, you've got to do something you never done before.

My friend, I had achieved something. I became the first boxer from the city of East St. Louis to reach the heights I had. It made me more than just a hometown hero, but an example to all who would follow after me. That desire and determination that fired within me took me to wherever I wanted to go. Over the years, after my defeat in the Olympics, I've remained positive by saying, "Shoot for the stars, for in doing so, if you miss, you will land in the clouds," and let me tell you, that ain't bad.

CHAPTER 8

Exile

After the Olympics LaTanya and I began to settle down and start our family. Shortly after we were married she was pregnant with our second child and in March of 1989 Areda Antoinette Johnson was born. Lakeisha now had a baby sister who would bring joy into our lives.

Shortly after getting home and settling down a bit I had to decide whether or not I wanted to become a professional boxer. At the time I was being supported by the Olympic Committee and they were sending my last check in the mail, so I had to decide quickly what I was going to do for money in order to take care of my family. While living in Minneapolis, I attended a church service where I heard a message that convinced my heart not to pursue a professional career. The sermon was about the young rich ruler, and as I listened to those words I allowed a conviction to condemn me to my career's death. I was a very young Christian and didn't have the faith and wisdom that develops over time. I saw myself that day as the young rich ruler; even though I wasn't rich yet, I had plans to become wealthy. After listening to this sermon, I felt I needed to retire from boxing. I do not think it was God's will for me to become convinced that I should retire. Knowing what I know now, I believe it was the negativity of the devil, who comes to steal, kill, and destroy lives, that crept into my thoughts and convinced me that I was not pursuing a Christian lifestyle. As I look back, I just needed someone to tell me that God never takes anything or asks anything from us that he will not replace with something better; I should never have become convinced that that I needed to quit what I was most passionate about.

I retired from boxing in December 1988. After my retirement I began to feel resentment and frustration about not giving a professional career a chance, but because of this conviction, I felt trapped. What I needed at this time was sound counseling, but I got everything except what I needed. I joined a church in Minneapolis that my mom and some of my siblings attended because it seemed to be the right place for me at the time. Since I thought I needed spiritual counseling, I approached a person who was a member of the church. I knew that this individual had been a Christian for much longer than I had and I felt he could help me. He was my advisor of sorts and we decided that we should fast and pray about the decisions I had to make concerning my livelihood at this particular time. After we fasted and prayed and came together to discuss my situation, it was determined by my advisor that God didn't want me boxing anymore. I personally felt that God had given me the O.K. to continue my career, but because of my youth in the Lord, I trusted someone else's opinions more than my own. This was a big mistake.

I've since then learned that God is the giver of all good things and certainly any talent comes from God, but because of the beliefs of the Christians with whom I surrounded myself, many were led to believe that it was evil for a Christian to be involved in any sporting arena. So there I was, feeling trapped, wanting to box, but felt I couldn't because perhaps God would allow something bad to happen to me. This caused me to get angry with God and feel frustrated with my life. I prayed, "If this is your will for my life, Lord, send something else my way," but it never happened. I must conclude that I now take full responsibility for my ignorance of not knowing the heart of God for my personal situation. After all, the decision was mine to make in terms of pursuing a professional career as a boxer. I think because I was on a level most people never reach in their entire lives, the advice given to me provoked much confusion. The people I looked to for spiritual advice had never been where I had been and I didn't want to accept the fact that maybe a little jealousy could have played a part in their advice.

I began to dislike everything around me. I was a very unhappy person as the days and months went by. All alone my wife kept saying, "If you believe God is with you, then he will be," but I was totally deaf to her wisdom because I valued the opinions of others more. This was my second mistake. My wife only wanted what was right for me. Meanwhile, all my Olympic teammates seemed to be doing great with the gifts they had.

The next several years became a living hell. I wish I would have taken my wife's wisdom, but as a foolish man, I thought she couldn't be right—maybe because she wasn't as well versed in the bible as these other people. This shouldn't have made a difference, but it did. *How did I ever get myself into this mess?* I wondered. Maybe if I never knew about Christianity I would not have had this challenge in my life. The mind is the ultimate battleground and that's where the most important victories are won and lost. I had no understanding of how to grasp hold to Jesus for myself, because I thought of myself as "a babe in Christ"—I had only been a Christian for two years.

It was as if I had been brain washed; the advice others gave me had me believing that they really had a one-on-one connection with God. I was at an all time low, yet I remained under the influence of their advice for a while. Then fear began to set in and to add to what I was going through, I began to experience every kind of attack from demons that you can't even imagine. I truly mean the real thing—not something that you see on television, but worse. I was convinced that the devil wanted me dead and it seemed as though he had me right where he wanted me: confused about everything, even God's love for me. But LaTanya stayed by my side praying that God would set me free by opening up my understanding. It was as if this situation completely ran my life and not God; I felt I had nowhere to turn to, not even to God.

As I think on it now, what a sad thing to experience. Many people are bound by the opinion of others and let me tell you, to use one's position in the Church to rule God's people and tell them to do what you think they should do, makes Christianity nothing short of being a cult religion. I remember one time waking up to a demonic figure on my pillow. I thought I was crazy! I realized that this situation was more than just out of hand, it was completely out of control. Deep down I had to believe that God would provide a way of escape for me, to resume my boxing career.

I've since learned that it's the advice of those who love you that matters and no one else, because those you love don't have hidden agendas. There are still many people today living in the dark ages who don't believe that prosperity is what God wants for his people, but perhaps it may be that we don't want it for each other. Throughout this experience the words I had said to my mother came back to haunt me. Though I never wanted to be back in the position I fought so hard to get out of, times got tougher and I needed public assistance and food stamps again in order to support my family. I remember going to apply at a place in downtown Minneapolis where I was recognized by the caseworker. He looked at me and said, "Man Arthur, you don't have to do this."

I said to my wife, "Tomorrow will be a brighter day," because something in me was still positive through it all. She couldn't figure out why I couldn't shake off these other Christians and move forward. Even when I prayed and fasted, there were differences of opinions about what I should do with my talents and potential career as a professional boxer. Although I felt God said "yes" to me, I didn't have enough confidence that it was He that put the "yes" in my spirit and not my own eagerness trying to pursue itself. I now know that the promises of God are "yes and yes indeed."

Contrary to most opinions of faith walkers, some feel that God gives three answers: "Yes," "No," and "Wait," but I've learned his answers are, "Yes," "Wait," or "I have something better for you."

There were times I really got the itch to fight again, but every time I allowed the advice of others to say, "It's not God's will." I remember calling my friend and former trainer, Jim, back in St. Louis. He had no idea what I had gotten myself into; I would tell him that I wanted to fight again, then I would consult with someone from the church, who would convince me otherwise, and I would call Jim back and say, "I don't think I really want to right now. I need more time to think about it," and he would accept it. Jim respected my decision, never knowing it wasn't my decision, but someone else's. I now know I was brain washed in the worst way. If you think brain washing doesn't occur in Christianity, you better think that over. I just didn't want to believe it because we are talking about serving the living God, the all knowing and supreme being of the universe. I wanted to think that those who chose to serve him were all of a clean heart and good intentions.

My wife kept persisting that I give boxing another try. Offers started to fade away the longer I stayed confused about my decision. As time went by this situation would have to take its course. I was in exile, away from common sense. It was as though I couldn't relate and couldn't be related to. Even family members, like some of my siblings, knew I was greatly depressed and basically watched me deteriorate from where I used to be. My confidence was no longer confidence, but doubt had opened its many doors for negative thoughts to enter. My mom wondered if I would resume my career, but she would let me decide for myself. She wanted what was best for me, but nobody knew how messed up I was except for my wife. I don't even think those who gave me their advice were aware of the awful pain and division in my soul that was brought upon me, which seemed to never end.

I've learned that man made Christianity has ruined more lives than any religious sect throughout our time here on earth. No one has the right to be or act as Lord over God's creation. As I continued to travel through this wilderness of depression, I worked a few jobs, never satisfied. I went back to school to pursue a career in broadcast journalism and I worked in the local school system for a couple years as a paraprofessional, child development technician, and an assisting principal. I later joined a multimillion-dollar insurance firm for a year, after graduating from broadcasting school in Minneapolis. I didn't pursue broadcasting as I had hoped because I was still influenced by the advice of others who told me it wasn't God's will.

Though I was trying to understand more about the Bible's real truth, it would need to take root, which wasn't happening at this point. I didn't know it then, but I do now, that the opinions of others had become a God to me. I accepted this advice as being from God. But my wife had wisdom and could see right through the advice of others and understood that they were not looking out for my best interest, but were jealous of me and my past accomplishments.

After getting to a point of almost being put out on the street because of my depression, I was driven to leave the jobs I had. I was intelligent enough to get a job, but I was miserable and I finally knew what I had to do. Suddenly, a boxing gym opened a couple of blocks from my house. It would be a little while before I would go there to work out, but it was as if God was saying, "This is where you belong, so I'm bringing it to you."

LaTanya and I had our third and final child, Arthur Anthony Johnson Jr. I remember praying over him, asking, "Lord, don't let him be nothing like me." I didn't like myself and hoped beyond hope that my son wouldn't have to experience the challenges I faced in my life. I hated that I had become a divided soul. One of the worst things that can happen to a person is to not be sure about anything. My wife was aware of the boxing gym around the corner and knew that God had answered her prayers, three years later.

I went to the gym without consulting anyone and worked out. After three years of not punching anything, it *felt* right. Though I was still in a state of confusion, as word got back to those who had been advising me not to box again, they tried to convince me again not to. But at this point in time I was going to do what I had to do to make myself and my family happy, no matter what. Finally.

CHAPTER 9

My Return to the Ring

People are most happy when they are chasing after their dreams—not when they have fulfilled them. At this point I fought to be happy with life again and slowly I began to try and do that. I discovered that if I was afraid to disagree with anyone, I would never succeed in life because part of succeeding will, at some point in time require disagreements. This time I decided to finally try to go all the way. I decided to make my return to the ring.

I made a couple of phone calls to Bill Jaffa, my boxing coach in Minneapolis, and to my dearest friend Jim. Bill may have had some inclination as to why my decision to return was halted. I recall him asking me, "Is the Padre the reason for your delayed return?" I never answered him because I never wanted to put anyone's name out for bad. Both coaches were elated that I had decided to resume my career, which was long overdue. From that point on I received no more calls and no more bother from the advisors I had previously sought. A tremendous amount of damage had been done to my life because I ignorantly allowed the understandings and advice of others.

I fasted and prayed for some five years for God to break the chains from my mind and spirit. Fasting two and three days a week, I had never faced a greater challenge than the battle to be free again. Now I understood what it meant to be free because I had been bound by man-made traditions and interpretations of what and who God is.

I had to learn how to be confident in my God given abilities as an athlete when that was the key to my success all along. The road back would be a long and weary one; I knew I had to take it one-step at a time, for the road to success begins with a single step. After training in Minneapolis for a while with Bill Jaffa, my wife and I made the decision that I would go and live with her mother in Centreville, Illinois, about 25 minutes from where I grew up. There I would be close to St. Louis, where Jim and I would meet to train. We also felt that I would be able to focus more on what I had to do to re-enter the world of boxing. Even though I was away from my family for long periods of time and missed them deeply, I knew this was a step toward making my dream of a professional career happen. Jim helped me work my body back into condition—I would have to get used to punching and being punched again. I got some work in prior to coming to train with Jim again by working out with my longtime teammate and friend, Cortez.

Cortez had moved to Minneapolis from Centreville, Illinois to stay with my family before getting settled, but he was busy living his own life and really didn't know how I suffered while living in Minneapolis. He thought it was good that I had retired for a while, but couldn't guess how I felt while retired. After hearing about my decision to return he was more than eager to help me in any way that he could. As time would have it Cortez and I started to drift farther apart. We had attended the same church in Minneapolis, where he was involved in the ministry. Eventually, he became very uninterested in that particular church and we just weren't as close as we had been growing up. We were young men now and our lives were going in different directions.

I continued forward with my boxing career and Jim and I decided I would need a manager. Angelo Dundee, the famous Hall of Fame trainer who managed people like the great Muhammad Ali and Sugar Ray Leonard, became my manager.

I had always been a dreamer and often imagined Dundee in my corner when I was growing up in the projects, as I shadow boxed in my room. LaTanya and our children moved back to Centreville with me; we decided to relocate back to Illinois since

I was going to be spending a lot of time there with my trainer as I started to prepare for my first professional bout. I was not yet signed with Angelo, but we were sure it would happen because he was the one working behind the scenes for my first bout. However, after a few cancellations I started to wonder if Jim and I had made the right decision because it seemed as though I was never going to have a debut.

In the midst of one of the cancellations, my mom had a relapse of breast cancer. This time it would cause her lungs to collapse. I was contacted and immediately flew home to see her. This was the beginning of her fight to live. My siblings and I did not know what awaited us in this battle for her life. After a few weeks my mom got better and I had to focus again in order to finally prepare for my debut.

Jim and I sharpened up a few things we had been working on and flew to Los Angeles, California. My brother Albert came to watch and to support me, since he lived nearby The Great Western Forum, where the Los Angeles Lakers basketball team played. My professional debut took place in this arena in May of 1992. I took on my first opponent, the undefeated Joe Monzano, who had three wins and no losses to his name. One year after starting to train again, I began my professional boxing career with a convincing win.

The celebration of my debut victory didn't last long. Shortly after this, tragedy struck unexpectedly. My mother had another relapse of the cancer that collapsed her lungs again. All we could do was to go see about her once again. My oldest brother Albert made the trip to see our mother from California to Minneapolis. Albert always enjoyed driving; I can remember from my little boy days Albert driving from California to East St. Louis to see the family after he left home whenever he had vacation time available. But this would be a very costly trip for him and his family, so they stayed for a few days to see our mom pull through. He and his wife and daughter headed back home. On the way back, driving through the night, Albert fell asleep and lost control of his car while driving through Colorado.

Afterwards, Albert explained that he awoke to find himself going at a high rate of speed across a field. He tried to slow down by hitting the breaks, but the car flipped and lost its roof top. He and his wife were badly injured, but even worse, their 6 year old daughter died from the trauma. It was terrible. After hearing about the accident, my mother became very remorseful, thinking that if he had not come to see her, this wouldn't have happened. She felt responsible for the loss of Albert's daughter. No one could have ever imagined something like that ever happening, but we knew that Albert would need our support to get through this.

We did what a family does, we met him and his wife in California a few days later. LaTanya and I, along with Stella and my niece Yvette (Albert's oldest daughter from his previous marriage) made the trip to console him and his wife. Albert's daughter's body would be flown from Colorado to California and it was one of the saddest funerals I ever attended. Her beautiful face had been disfigured by the trauma and we could hardly recognize her. After staying some days with them we drove back to Illinois, where things would once again began to settle down a bit. We stayed in touch with Albert and Sabrina until they could stand on their own again and I began to try and refocus on my career.

I fought for the second time as a professional in St. Louis where I knocked out my opponent in the first round. Although I didn't receive much money for my first two bouts (having received $600 for the first and $500 for the second), I was sure the money would come eventually. Money wasn't a huge issue at this time because Jim was also sponsoring me with the agreement that I would pay him back. We trusted each other for years, afterall, when I bought my first home in Minneapolis, Jim loaned me the money for my down payment until I could pay him back.

Another guy came into the picture named Bill Martin, who wanted to buy five percent of my professional boxing career, which meant he would be entitled to five percent of my future contracts to fight. We agreed that he would take on the sole responsibilities of sponsoring me throughout my professional career. But before that deal could be worked out, Jim and I had to make the trip to Florida to visit Angelo Dundee, since he was our first choice of manager. Immediately after meeting Angelo, I worked out and I sparred a few rounds; after seeing me in action, Angelo decided that he wanted to work with me. He felt that I was a very good prospect, so we signed a contract to make him my manager. I didn't receive any money for signing because I was expected to earn my money by winning my way to a world title.

When we returned from signing with Angelo Dundee, I signed with Bill Martin for five percent of my career. The deal was sealed with a $50,000 check made out to me. Troubles seemed far behind, yet ever so near. Bill Martin was a business man who knew how to make money. He was a stock broker at a very large investment firm, but he enjoyed taking risks.

I once asked him, "What made you sure that I might succeed?"

Bill said, "Arthur, I'm a big risk taker. What must be understood here is that nothing is a guarantee."

Little guys in boxing, like I was, don't make the millions like heavyweights. Even though we have the opportunity to make nice money, $50,000 is certainly a high risk when sponsoring a flyweight because an injury could easily occur that would eliminate the chance to make back that signing bonus. The risk certainly had to be taken into consideration by both me and Bill Martin. I would have to prove that I was the real thing as a professional.

Despite the new contracts, I still had doubts. Even though things seemed to be going well, I still had many battles that awaited. My mind was still the main battleground and convincing myself to believe that God was with me, was difficult. I wanted to know prior to becoming a Christian that God would be directing my path. Herein lay the challenge of my faith. Even though I had had two successful professional bouts, I still fought with a divided spirit that caused me to feel conflicted about my presence in the ring. Just entering a ring under those circumstances was hell within itself.

What I was experiencing was not easily broken because the ministry in which I was a part of in Minneapolis did not agree with Christian athletes and this had become such a large part of my spiritual understanding. When I returned to the area I contacted Clara, who still lived in East St. Louis, and she promised that she would continue to pray for me. I was encouraged to join a church that was right across the street from my mother-in-law's house, which served as a healing virtue for me. I became active in the ministry again, which really felt good and it was a great change from what I was involved in before. Ministry is certainly more than being behind a pulpit. As I understood it, I could work in other areas of ministry until my healing was complete. It would take years before I ever wanted to serve behind any church pulpit.

It would be a battle fighting demonic spirits or negative thoughts on a regular basis, pleading the blood of Jesus. I really felt downright uncomfortable. I often said, "God, why me? Why couldn't I have gone ahead and turned pro earlier like my Olympic teammates did?" They were much farther along than I was and I had to make up for four years worth of lost time. I hated the fact that I moved to Minneapolis and that I ever met those Christians, but all the same I had to find it in my heart to forgive and move on. It wasn't that simple. So many doors were opened for negativity to come in and fight with my mind. My greatest fight was always the fight to be free.

I focused on my career and I started to pile up victories and move into the world rankings. Things got better a little bit at a time and I had to cling to the faith that said, "God freely gives us all things." I continued to win as Hall of Fame boxing champions like Joe Frazier (known by fight fans as Smokin' Joe) and Muhammad Ali came out to watch and support me. Wow, the greatest came to see me in action. These were athletes I most definitely admired as I was growing up, watching them on television with my once little boy's eyes.

As things got even better, by 1993 I was in line for my first world title opportunity in the flyweight division, weighing 112 pounds. I beat the current world champion of the International Boxing Council in only my fourth bout. It was an eight round decision, non-title fight against Richard Clark. I had only fought in seven professional bouts, so that within itself was an accomplishment. The only other American fighter to do that was Leon Spinks when he fought Ali. It just doesn't happen in America because managers want a lot of easier bouts for their fighters before putting them in for a title bout. My situation was different in that I had a huge amount of experience as an amateur, but this kind of victory was not at all the norm except for in European boxing.

I had the goods and everybody in the boxing arena knew it. Being ranked number five in the world was all that was needed to convince the champion's manager that they wanted to fight me. I had not had many pro bouts and had never been past eight rounds in my career, so they felt because of the lack of pro experience they should be able to beat me easily.

Meanwhile on more than one occasion my mother's condition grew worse. I remember once driving my sister Stella there to spend time with her. Throughout the duration of her illness I remember driving back home from Minnesota and crying every mile of the drive. I now knew it was a matter of time. While spending time in Minneapolis with my mother, we had many conversations. She would ask me to sing "Amazing Grace," for she loved to hear me sing. As I sang it, tears rolled down her face and she knew that the time was drawing near for her to touch the face of God. Though we hoped for a miracle, the cancer had spread. It was now in her lungs and it seemed that the harder I prayed, the worse she got. I kept thinking, *If I could just bring a faith healer to her.* But I knew none. Then I thought, *God if I had the gift of healing I could heal her.* These thoughts and more rolled through my mind as I drove back to Cahokia, Illinois were I now lived with my family.

CHAPTER 10

Saying Goodbye:

My Mother Loses Her Fight

I flew to Minneapolis to see my mother in the hospital as the doctors said that there was nothing more they could do for her. The cancer had spread to her brain cells, so they were thinking of sending her home. As I made my way to her room at the hospital I saw the spirit of death upon her as she looked at me and said, "I want to go home. Don't let them keep me here any longer." At this point she was very incoherent at times but all the same, her wishes would be respected by the family. As we took her home I remember it being very cold and it was now a matter of days and hours. I asked God when this painful situation would come to an end and He responded in a vision to me. I later understood that it would end the day that I picked her up from her bedroom floor.

Saying goodbye to someone I've known my whole life was the most difficult thing I ever had to do. This woman that I knew as Mom, whom for many years my siblings and I called "Madear," short for "Mother Dear," was shrunken down to merely flesh and bones. The suffering was like nothing I had ever seen and most certainly something I never want to witness again. I heard a friend of the family say, "Maybe she wouldn't have suffered long if she had not fought it back so hard." Perhaps this person was trying to look on a brighter note, but all the same I say you've only got one life to live and that's worth fighting for.

In those last days spent with her we hoped and prayed many times for a miracle until the very end. Throughout her suffering I never heard her complain once about her situation; she just took it as it came. I remembered way back to my childhood when she stood up all alone against the big bullies when we lived in East St. Louis. I thought back to all the times she tried to teach me and my siblings how to live like respectable people. I couldn't help but remember that this was the woman who disciplined me, gave advice to me, supported my decisions, and loved me. This brave woman, even after becoming a Christian, still had the same warrior characteristics she developed when we lived in the projects. She showed us all how to die with dignity.

The morning of her departure I found her lying on her bedroom floor. I went into her room to check on her and found that she was trying to get to a chair so she could sit upright. Later, as I and one of my siblings helped her way back to the bed, she requested that her pillows be placed in an upright position. We didn't know why she always wanted to be in a sitting up position instead of lying down, but as we all discovered when we looked back on the situation that she wanted to meet death face to face. It was as if she said within herself, "I'm not going without a fight. If you're going to take me, well you're going to have to take me staring you in the face." I understood when I picked her up from the bedroom floor that it was to be the end. God had spoken to me in the midst of my very painful situation. I learned that God truly cares, no matter what you may be faced with, in the hour you feel that no one is concerned, He proves His love.

The morning she passed away I heard her take her last breath from the room right next door. I shall always remember the sound; it was a death rattle, the sound of a loud, last breath taken as she passed away. The ambulance arrived first and the paramedic asked how long she had been without oxygen and if we wanted her to be revived. As the paramedic stared me in the face, my answer was, "No, because it was her request not to be." All the family members were notified and as many as could come, came to the house before she was carried away by the funeral hearse. My brother Albert made it back for the funeral as well. He never blamed our mother for losing his daughter a year earlier. He accepted it as he had to, as an unforeseen circumstance and painfully moved on. Our family gathered and found the strength to get through.

During this time I felt even more sorrowful for my sister Pearlina and my brother Calvin because of their disabilities. Calvin continued to stay in a group home, which was arranged years before my mother's passing. Pearlina had come to stay with our mother after her husband died, but would now live with our sister Regina. Since there was a 20 year gap between me and my oldest sibling, perhaps I was much too young to recall Pearlina's disability, especially since it wasn't the sort of thing that got talked about in our household growing up. Now I was able to understand more clearly Pearlina's challenges and the kind of care and attention she and Calvin needed.

While I cut my brother Calvin's hair in preparation for the funeral, he said to me, "She will come back." I became even more broken inside because I knew his understanding was limited. I remember Calvin praying over our mom once saying, "God heal her in her last days here on earth," for it affected him in the worst way.

As we prepared for the funeral I was notified that my brother James had gotten into some drug related trouble and he was not going to be able to attend his mother's funeral to say goodbye. For him I wept, because even though he made the wrong choices,

I just thought it was sad that he wasn't going to be able to say his farewells.

At the funeral I sang "Farther Along We Will Understand Why" as the preacher gave the eulogy and our family viewed her body for the last time. A nephew placed a rose on her. Sobbing painfully as we sat down after the viewing, I remember my baby girl Areda, whispering to me, "Dad she's only sleeping." It was the voice of God through the mouth of a child. I recognized that my mom was greatly loved by family and friends that she touched while living as a woman of God.

To this day I run into old friends and they say, "Your mother was as sweet as sweet can be." The family rallied around Calvin to give support and my brother Albert offered to take him to California for awhile to stay. Unfortunately this couldn't work because Albert was unable to give him the care he required. So Calvin was able to get back into the group home in Minneapolis. As I had promised my mother that I would make sure he would be taken care of, I accepted the responsibility to be Calvin's guardian. Through it all I've learned that when you have a good mother, nothing ever takes the place of that. You've only got one, appreciate her while she lives. Take out the time to say, "I love you."

One of the most difficult things for a human being to do is to say, "I love you." Why is that? It's not practiced enough and I am so thankful I told my mom countless times that I loved her. I can still hear her voice say, "When you have honored your parents, God will always let his sun shine upon you." I began to get closer to my dad, even though there were perhaps some discrepancies between us. But we would begin to work through them all.

CHAPTER 11

God Loves a Good Fight

A few weeks after my mother's passing, I continued to prepare myself for my first title shot, amazingly enough, I was able to stay focused and keep training while I was in Minneapolis for my mom. Of course that was very difficult for me, but the contract had been signed and I had to keep going. I'm just thankful I didn't have to pull out of the fight under these extreme circumstances. My mom wouldn't have wanted me throwing in the towel. I recall her once saying to me during her last stay at the hospital that she knew I would come to see her, even if I had to crawl on my knees and hands. She knew what she meant to me, but some of my family members felt it was too soon for me to return to the ring. But I was certain that my mother would be looking down from her heavenly throne, cheering me on.

I was avid about moving forward because I was sure of my faith in God and knew that He would give me the strength and courage to get the job done. Upon my return to Cahokia, Jim and I went over ring strategies by getting the final bit of sparring I needed.

The time had come for my return to boxing and the challenge was indeed at hand. After having competed in only seven professional bouts at this time, I was now in a position to be a world champion in spite of everything I had been through. My manager and I, as well as Jim, were confident I was talented enough to overcome any obstacle my opponent threw at me. My wife and family stayed behind as I headed to Bangkok Thailand, to challenge the World Champion, Pichit Sitbanprochan for his International Boxing Federation title in January 1994.

It was an experience I will never forget. Met at the airport by their countrymen, the stage was set for a memorable 12 round championship bout. As we drove through Bangkok, we saw billboards depicting me and my opponent. It was clearly going to be a hugely watched match.

My luggage didn't arrive with me, so I went to jog and gather the temporary equipment we bought after arriving in Thailand. I was smothered by reporters, it took a day to finally get our luggage. I had a few light workouts before the fight and then it was time for the weigh ins. We were bombarded by more reporters and fans as we entered and I was greeted by the Thailand's world champion.

More than 70,000 people turned out to watch this fight, including Thailand's Prime Minister and other dignitaries. I proved to be more than just a threat, but Pichit was awarded an undeserving decision. I never felt 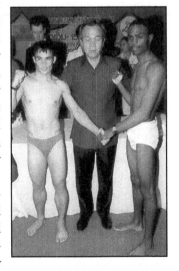 more deeply hurt than I did at that moment. Politics, once again, had played a huge roll in my career since the Olympics. Even though I received thousands of dollars for my efforts in Thailand, I went there for more than the money. It helped that many people who didn't even speak English let me knew they felt I had gotten robbed.

On my way back to the hotel, I saw Bill Brennan, the head commissioner of the International Boxing Federation. I was in a complete state of shock and didn't pay much attention to him, but Jim told me later that Mr. Brennan said, "Arthur, you may have won that fight, but not tonight."

This title was organized by and American-based Federation and you would have thought that they would want the title back on U.S. soil. A win in Thailand would have given me the privilege of becoming the first African American Flyweight champion. But I had a lot to learn about sanctioning fees, which is money paid to the I.B.F. every time the champion fights. Sometimes promoters, such as Pichit's, were very generous with their sanctioning fees and, unfortunately, this had everything to do with Pichit keeping his title that night. After fighting my heart out, only to hear that the head commissioner of the I.B.F. himself thought that I should have won, it was unbearable. I quietly took it in as my trainer Jim's facial expression said it all. This defeat made my mother's passing a few weeks earlier hurt just a tad bit more.

Pichit's career was changed forever after this match; he only fought once more because he retired due to brain damage. It was obvious that I was responsible for that. Anything that goes terribly wrong in a fight like a brain injury is certainly accidental. No fighter ever wants to cause permanent damage to another, only temporary pain in order to secure a victory. Although you must have a killer instinct, at the end of the day anything that goes seriously wrong is totally unwelcomed. I knew the business I was entering was a very serious one in which I could be hurt.

Everyone knew that I gave him the worst beating of his career; my manager Angelo highly agreed.

Even while competing at this level, the confusion and division of my spirit lingered. At the fight in Thailand, it felt as if God lifted a yoke so that I could compete well and give a good account of myself. I remembered a prophecy spoken to me while living in Minneapolis; the prophet said that God was going to give me what my heart was yearning and desiring for. Even in my loss, He proved faithful. If there's one thing about God that I've learned, it's that he watches over his word and performs it. The battle ground of my mind still had to be won at this point and my response was continually, "Why me?"

I was reminded of a story that Jim once told me about the famous tennis star Arthur Ashe. After he learned he had AIDS by way of a blood transfusion, he said to a reporter, "Many people say when bad things happen to them, 'why me?' But I say, 'why not me?'" I remembered that I was greatly blessed and had been given a second chance to make my heart's desire come true. I was given the grace to go after a professional boxing world title, and even though I didn't win it on my first attempt, I was sure that if I kept at it, one day I could.

After my first attempt in the championship bout, I came home and rested for a few weeks before going back into training. I can't stress enough about being bothered by the chains that bound me. I'm not one to point a finger at any particular denominational group, but I must say that my experience with certain Christian traditions left me scarred for many years. For that matter I could have been a Pentecostal, Baptist, or Catholic, because the main issue involved here is the fact that the human race is entirely negative and unbelieving. Sure, I thank God for my liberty now, but my liberty then was man's analogy of what God was like. Understanding what the will of the Father is imperative for anyone who trusts his guidance.

I prepared for my next bout, four months later, held in Los Angeles, California. Once again I would fight at the Great Western Forum Auditorium where many celebrities often attended to see championship boxing at its best. My opponent was Alberto

Jimenez, who was ranked second in the world by many of the top organizations in boxing. He had over 35 wins and only one defeat, I had only eight pro bouts. Jimenez had even more bouts than the champion I fought in Thailand, and he was definitely not short of experience.

I remember this fight distinctively because it was one of the fights in which I still battled the condemnation issues. The devil was not intending to let me accomplish my goals without a challenge. As I entered the ring that night I was a very disturbed young soul; times before, God had lifted the burden, but this time I would suffer through it. A celebrity sang the National Anthem and the crowd roared. I felt all alone even though my trainer was present. My family cheered from home, watching it on television.

The moment had arrived for me to do my job and it would be yet another memorable fight witnessed on the Fox network. The deciding winner of this fight would go on for another title shot. We fought in close quarters; neither of us wanted to budge an inch. I fought in a confused emotional state as I often did; wondering how was I able to do that. This fight went right down to the wire. Jimenez was by far the toughest opponent I would meet as a professional. As we battled tooth and nail to the end of the last sounding bell, and as a crowd of thousands stood on their feet to cheer, the ten round decision was about to be announced. We waited quietly to hear that by one point on one of the three judge's score cards, a split decision verdict for Jimenez. His hand was raised; that was a hard pill to swallow. This was my second straight loss.

Now the pain that I endured for this bout began to hurt just that much more. The swollen face and bruised hands would take some time to heal. On the next morning Jim and I flew home together and Jim stressed how proud he was of my huge heart. I battled even after being hurt a couple of times in the fight by the sharp punches my opponent threw. My wife and family and those who saw the fight that night continued to encourage me.

The greatest encouragement came the next morning after I had gotten home. I heard a voice speak to my spirit, saying,

"Cast not away therefore your confidence." As I awoke, my lips continued to utter the words, "Cast not away therefore your confidence." I called Clara, my mentor, godmother, and woman of spiritual guidance to tell her what I had experienced during that morning. She replied, "Son that's scripture, turn to Hebrews 10:35 in your Bible," and there it was, just as it had been spoken to my spirit. I wasn't aware of that particular scripture because I was still learning and being healed. She said to me,"Son always remember that scripture God gave you. It will be your weapon against future attacks on your mind."

Now I knew he was on my side because of the great visitation. The adversary would continue to fight, but now I had more confidence. The interesting thing about this situation was that I had felt forsaken before the bout with Jimenez, but an assurance from God made my defeat bearable. Jimenez would go on to win a world title in his next fight and would reign as the World Boxing Organization champion for a good length of time before losing it to a European fighter. But the night he and I fought was one for the keeping, a fight in which I believe God Himself enjoyed.

God sent His words of encouragement to build me up, just like in the days of David when God told him to pursue the enemy. Not that God takes sides; I'm sure Jimenez prayed that night as I did. As I saw it, it was now his time to reign, but leave no room for doubt—God certainly likes a good fight. Whatever struggles you may be faced with, never give up, no matter what. This is a rule that I now teach my children: I can accept it if you try and fail, but I can never accept it if you never try.

CHAPTER 12

The Spirit of Insanity:

My Forty Days and Forty Nights

As my training schedule resumed after the Jimenez fight, I received a phone call late in the night that my sister Theresa's sixteen year old son had been found drowned in a lake in Minnesota. It struck like déjà vu, as if I had seen it before in a vision, and my heart dropped. Only 6 months after my mother's passing, now Joshua. He was only a kid and like a second son to me. My life was turned inside out and it seemed to knock the wind right out of me. It was reported that a fisherman found him in the lake after he was murdered by gang members. I knew I had to be strong for my family because they would look to me for strength. I made the trip to Minneapolis, this time going alone as my wife and children stayed behind. When I got there I was greeted with hugs by my family; we all were in amazement. I would console Theresa throughout my stay because for a mother to lose a child it has to be one of the hardest things to experience.

My mind reflected on this young life; Joshua was gone before his time like the wind that whispered in the night, gone by morning light.

I don't know if the law enforcement ever caught the responsible parties. We were never notified that anyone was brought to justice for this act of crime, even though nothing was going to ever bring him back. He left behind one older brother and one younger sister, as well as his mother. The situation became big news across the airways, but I'm thankful that the press was kind enough not to bother the family by allowing us to grieve privately. When the funeral took place I was glad to see my brother James, who was now out of trouble and had made it to the funeral to offer support to our sister.

As unexpected as this was, I learned as my mom taught me: there are no guarantees—you are here today and you could be gone tomorrow. Life would be changed forever for Theresa, but with much support she would find the strength to continue to move forward for her other two children.

I often think about Joshua, what his life would have been like and what he would have been. I know those thoughts often came to his mother and no matter how much you pray, time is the only thing that will eventually heal. I headed back home some days later, sadden by this tragedy. I needed peace of mind and for no other deaths to take place in my family. This had been enough for a life time. I noticed the parallels in the history of our family's tragedy. My mother lost a daughter early, my brother Albert lost his daughter, and now Theresa's son was gone from us too. Their pain was unbearable. Getting back to normal seemed a lot harder because now I kept thinking, *What's next?* Paranoia began to set in and I was shaken by simple things.

An anchor of strength came, not overnight, but in time. I kept moving forward and I wish I could tell you that God instantly made everything alright, but it didn't happened that way. I had to learn to trust and not to fear because fear is a tormenting factor that will destroy your life if you don't take control over it. We all have our own personal fears, but I learned that I must face my greatest fears, for in doing so, the threats of things that may happen began to fade away.

I had a few bouts that I won convincingly, which put me back in contention for my second world title shot. This time I was up against an old foe I had fought in the amateurs and defeated: Johnny Tapia. He was the reigning super bantam weight champion, at 115 pounds, which was 3 pounds higher than the flyweight division. My team and I decided to move up in weight to challenge the champ. I was respected in that division, as was Tapia, and his team didn't have to fight me because I wasn't a mandatory challenge. However, in order to get networks to air the champion's bout, Tapia would have to fight a reputable opponent. My manager was great at making things like that happen for me because he knew how. Dundee had experience with guys like Ali, Sugar Ray Leonard, George Foreman and many others, but before this bout could take place, I had another battle to face both physically and spirtually.

I was back on a winning track, but the battle waging inside my mind was not nearly over yet. The next ten months would prove incredibly difficult. With all I had achieved, condemnation still lingered. It was a feeling of guilt for continuing to pursue my career in boxing. I shouldn't have felt guilty about using my talents to become successful. But this is the major weapon the devil uses against God's children.

The problem was that the Christian world in which I was accustomed did not produce a lot of success stories. Most Christians I knew were not successful. I became a hope for those who knew me, someone for them to look at as an example of success. Those who wanted to support me, didn't, because of fear, perhaps because they didn't think success should exist for Christians. This is why many of my friends were reluctant about joining the church. Since most felt as though they couldn't succeed at what their hearts desired, it was as if jealousy was a permissible way to deal with others' success. It was like reading a rule book that focused exclusively on all the things I couldn't do, which is exactly what I was afraid of when I began my journey with Christ. Those Christians who I allowed to influence me were evidence of men seeking man's approval instead of God's, which is the worst kind of bondage I could have experienced.

So I had to be particular about who I sought advice from because I couldn't understand how people felt that they could advise me if they hadn't walked the path I was on. During this time God spoke to my spirit, saying I would walk on grounds were never a man had walked before. So I had to seek advice now from those who had my best interest at heart. It didn't matter whether they were Christians or not because the fact is, God is the God of all flesh—He can send direction for your life through a television commercial if He chooses to.

I came to learn that boxing is one of those things most people enjoy watching. Maybe people like it because it reminds us of life in general: its ups and downs, its setbacks and comebacks. Because of the glamour and many other things that are involved which shouldn't matter, some particular Christians often described boxing by saying, "It's worldly." Some thought I wasn't really a Christian, even though I had confessed and given my testimony, because I had managed to gain some success for myself. I always saw this point of view to be judgmental and narrow minded. From my perspective, a man falls away when he is enticed by his own lust, but I never saw boxing as a problem that could take away my salvation. I've learned I was right, but those who challenged me disfigured my judgment.

The name of this spirit I struggled with was insanity and I carried it around for years. Leaving Minnesota brought sheer hell. I can recall it as if it had happened yesterday. The pinnacle of my ordeal brought uncontrollable thoughts that I could not break free from. Every vile thing you can imagine entered my mind and all I could do was to try to maintain some sanity as this spirit entered my home. Despite all of the praying and rebuking, it had to take its course.

In the early stages of this attack my wife was aware of this war within me. I called her at work to tell her that I was going to admit myself into the hospital, the suffering was more than I could bear. I heard her begin to weep on the other end of the phone as she agreed. When I hung up the phone the Holy Spirit spoke to me and said, "Rebuke the evil spirit," and as I did I began to feel a sense of ease, but every time I would let up, it came back even stronger. The day progressed slowly and as my wife got home from work I called on the praying warrior, Mother Johnson. She was just preparing to eat her dinner when she sensed a cry for help.

She said, "Son, come and get me now. We are going to have prayer in your home and bind the enemy up." I went and picked her up and brought her to my house where we began to pray. She laid her hands on my head and I fell as if I was a dead man onto my living room floor. Clara and LaTanya continued to pray over me. Later as time went by there were days that I remember things moving without anyone touching them and a strong, stinking odor, which was indescribable. The spirit of fear gripping me as never before, I saw visions of myself lying in the kitchen floor in my home with my siblings and family gathered around.

Days passed and I became very angry with God asking, "Why are you allowing this to happen to me? Do you want my wife to be a widow?!" After my bitter response to Him I heard His voice speak clearly to me. In that instance He said, "Where were you when I formed the world?" and I quickly repented. I can't say that I didn't falter throughout this situation, because I did, big time. I constantly repented to God, admitting that I was an imperfect human being who is subject to failure at times. As I look back, even though I fought God, He was letting me know by responding to me that He was in control.

I continued to fight and there were times that I felt as if there was a yoke tied around my neck. When I slept at night it was as if this spirit was trying to suffocate me, but I had to keep rebuking it in the name of Jesus, by his shed blood at the cross, and the name of Jesus alone would be enough to get me through this nightmare. Amazingly enough throughout this ordeal I continued to train, never speaking a word of it to my trainer. I was convinced he would never understand. Even to this day I've never spoken a word of it to him.

Finally I began to feel free. Each passing day got just a little easier. I kept track of the time I spent going through this and found that it was forty days and forty nights. I had paid a price to be free from this evil spirit and it was not easy. I would never wish this upon my worst of enemies. I suppose this ordeal is something that may be hard for anyone to imagine and one might even think I was involved with witchcraft or something of its kind. My response is never, no way. God allowed me to go through this experience so that I could free myself from the incredible amount of negativity and ill intentions that had surrounded my life for so many years.

I do not tell this story to magnify the devil, but to expose him. Testimonies such as this one need to be heard instead of allowing movie theatres to teach us about the works of the devil in horror movies. Christian success stories need to be heard, whether from an athlete in a sporting arena or a politician who holds public office. These two areas continue to shape our society and Christians should present themselves and their stories as real people who happen to be successful.

Mother Clara Johnson was a very strong support for me along with my wife during this time and for that, I will always be grateful. I learned that condemnation stems from religion and man-made traditions. I must tell you that the type of religion that relies on these tactics is demonic. When it was all over God promised me that condemnation would be like a plant on a house top, having no root. The promise would hold true. God separated me from religion and I began to meet other Christians who had not been taught the way I had. And they were successful, as a matter of fact. What I had been through seemed to be foolishness to them, and they were right.

CHAPTER 13

Getting Back on Track

I now felt that I was on an equal playing field with my opponents. I would no longer enter the ring divided, but more focused than ever. Now I was free from man's spiritual opinions and I resumed training for my second opportunity to become championship of the world. In order to win that title, I would have to get past Narsico Rodriguez from the Dominican Republic. At the Great Western Forum auditorium in Los Angeles, the fight between me and Rodriguez turned out to be very one sided in my favor. I defeated him convincingly, which brought me an opportunity that I did not foresee, but not without a cost of an old hand injury which would seem to plague me throughout preparation for my challenge.

The fight for the world championship title would be against Johnny Tapia and would take place on his home turf in Albuquerque, New Mexico. I trained in Lacrosse, New Mexico to get acclimated to the high altitude. The stage was set for Johnny and me to be seen in millions of homes on ABC's Wide World of Sports on July 3rd, 1995. The ABC network helped to bring me into millions of homes by this time, which gave me the notoriety of being one of the greatest amateurs of all times. As the bout with Tapia approached, my aim was to make good on this second chance, because I had loss in my first opportunity to hold a world title in Thailand. While many great fighters all over the world never even get one opportunity, no matter how talented they were. This second chance was something to be thankful for.

When I first turned pro my attitude was, "If I fail, I fail," but now I was in a different frame of mind. I never wanted to look back and say what I could have done and what I should have done. I wanted no regrets, because regrets harbor bitterness that can undoubtedly affect the heart. I found myself once again in the spot light, trying to achieve my heart's desire. It made no difference where the fight was held; after going through what I had been through, I was willing to go to Tapia's house or fight in his backyard to de-throne him. That's how much I believed in my ability to get the job done. Johnny and I were well acquainted from our amateur days, having split one win against each other out of the two bouts we had in our early careers. He was well aware that I was a man on a mission and very unsure about allowing me the opportunity to fight for his title. But ABC network television only broadcasts the best in worldwide competition. The promoter, Bob Arum, was very aware that such a highly matched fight could make a lot of money for the fighters and the promoters, so this one had to happen.

I was just as big and solid as Tapia and maybe stronger. We weighed in as super bantam weights at 115 pounds. Johnny and I spoke briefly. We both knew it was to be business as usual. As tensions mounted high, I was not going to be denied the honor of becoming champion of the world.

Announcer Michael Buffer made his famous declaration, "Let's get ready to rumble!" and the Johnson auditorium in Albuquerque became electrified. This crowd would be the most hostile crowd I ever fought in front of; thousands of Mexicans came to cheer on their Mexican hero, Tapia, but all the same I was not to be shaken. I was familiar with huge crowds (I had Thailand to thank for that) and this auditorium was packed to its capacity of more than 16,000 yelling fans.

It lived up to its expectation of a great fight. Some of the greatest matches on record have been between African Americans and Mexicans and this one was a reminder of such. At the end of the rival, the decision was ready to be announced. I was sure of a win, considering I had knocked him down on two occasions. But they were not counted as knock downs, though it was clear that a punch put him down and not a slip of his footing, as the referee called them. The rules of boxing allow the judges to score from their own perspective. I had faith that the judges would side in my favor.

Michael Buffer announced a split decision and the crowd roared. I thought, "Mission accomplished!" only to hear him say that Johnny Tapia was declared the winner. My heart dropped as I saw my wife, mother in law, dad, and friends who made the trip to support me. Our children stayed behind to witness one of boxings most unbelievable decisions, live on television.

As I made my way out of the ring I heard a Mexican fan say something about the T-shirt I was wearing. I had a shirt with a picture of my mom on it and I dedicated the fight to her memory. A rowdy fan yelled out, "Forget that dead bitch!" There are no words for the amount of anger I held in my heart at that moment. Before any kind of reaction could boil to the surface, I was distracted by my manger Angelo and trainer Jim to get inside of my locker room.

After the bout I had to go to the press conference, where Johnny and I saw each other for the last time. Sitting there was Bob Arum, who thought it was hilarious that I came away empty handed. He was Johnny's promoter, and as I had learned earlier about promoters, I was once again a victim of circumstances. After the press conference I went immediately to the hospital to get my eye taken care of by the physician, since I managed to get a cut just above the left eye during the fight. I was driven back to my hotel room where I would finally get the chance to shower. I was too sore to even pull off my clothes in order to shower but somehow managed.

I said to my wife, "I refuse to let man kill my spirit." She looked at me with tender care and replied, "Don't let them baby."

Later in the evening we went down to get a bite to eat in the hotel restaurant. We saw the ring announcer, Mr. Buffer, who explained that Bob Arum had him read the final scoring differently from the score cards he was given. Mr. Buffer said that he really didn't want to do it, but he had no say in the matter. Originally, it was scored a draw, which meant Tapia would have kept his title anyway because a title can't change hands on a draw. It was announced as such to the crowd before the split decision verdict. Those who watched from around the world even thought I out performed him, which was a huge accomplishment, because to get a draw in the home town of the champion, indeed means that I was the true winner.

A draw wasn't good enough for Mr. Arum, so the decision had to be changed in Tapia's favor entirely. It was changed right there on national television, in front of everyone watching. People came up to me after that fight when I got home and kept saying, "I can't believe they did that on national television!"

After talking with Mr. Buffer I looked up and saw the officials at the same restaurant. I wanted to go over to just shake their hands as a good gesture, but as I made my way over to do that, one of the officials responded to me out of a guilty conscience and said, "If you have any disagreements about the decision, you need to take that up with the organization." God has given each of us a conscience. Even when we do things we know that we shouldn't do, it whips us inside. I suppose me going over to shake their hands was like me heaping coals of fire on their conscience. That honestly wasn't even on my mind as I was only going over to shake their hands, even though they were part of a conspiracy. I suppose that is just the type of person I am, always showing respect to my fellow man as I had been taught from my youth.

CHAPTER 14

Refusing No for an Answer:
The North American Title

When everyone around you tries to make you believe that your goals are impossible, it's time to start refusing to take "No" for an answer.

It was extremely hard to win a World championship because I did not have a promoter. My manager Angelo thought we could win the title without a promoter's help, but that proved to be close to impossible. Promoters are the deciding factors of the sport, but I felt when I stepped into that ring anything could happen and a promoter couldn't save anyone from being knocked out. Faith is the ingredient that holds everything together. My desire grew stronger than ever, but I learned that sometimes you can't achieve your desire unless you're willing to die for it. Many goals aren't accomplished because people aren't willing to give up absolutely everything to realize their dreams. There's a saying I firmly believe in: "Those who say winning isn't everything are the ones who never won anything."

After yet another disappointing loss, hard work awaited me. My bout with Johnny Tapia was my third loss out of the fifteen fights I had as a pro. Johnny's record held a huge number of fights against mine, but my amateur experience helped to cancel out any edge he thought he had. Before I could fight again I suffered through a drought for months of inactivity, mainly because the top competition refused to compete unless it was mandatory. Ten and a half months later, Angelo was able to get me an opportunity with the forum boxing promoters in California. A promoter named Tony Curtis felt they could give me an opportunity to fight against topnotch competitors, which I most certainly welcomed after a long layoff.

I fought in a nationally televised bout in Reno, Nevada against Antonio Ruiz. This was the beginning of a good relationship with Forum Promotions, since I defeated Ruiz with ease. After dropping back down to the flyweight division, we had an agreement by integrity with Forum Promotions that they would keep me active. If I were to become a mandatory defense for a world title opportunity, they would be given the first opportunity to promote it. So Forum worked together with Angelo to give me a chance to work my way back into contention.

I was in line to fight for another major title in the fall of 1996 with the North American Boxing Federation, which most certainly could lead to another World title opportunity. I don't think that the current champion had plans on giving up his title, because he wanted the chance at a world title as well. I believe he took the chance of fighting me because he felt he could beat me. I don't believe a man enters a war knowing he's going to lose—only a fool does that.

As the fight approached it was tougher for me to lose the extra weight I was carrying in order to get back down to the flyweight division, but I managed to take my body through the necessary changes to get there. Fighting for the North American title is every bit as reputable as a world title, as a matter of fact it is one of the longest lineages in boxing history, dating as far back as the Ali Era. I remember watching tapes of Ali fighting Ken Norton for the right to be called the North American Heavyweight Champion. Ali's career was full of comebacks, some feel one too many, but I say he did what he felt he had to do.

I entered the ring before the champion, as is the custom in boxing. Makito Martinez, another Mexican flyweight, entered the ring last. This fight took place in the champion's hometown, at the

Great Western Forum in Los Angeles. I was convinced a change was coming and as the national anthem was belted out, the huge crowd erupted.

The bell rang, signaling the first round, which was an all out war for both of us, neither wanting to take a step back. The second round would bring even more action, until I put him down with a crushing right hand. He got up, only to be put down by a left hook. Still determined, he got up again and that's when I threw everything at him and the referee had no choice but to call the fight to a halt.

I won the title in a second round knockout. It was surprising to many because I had never displayed my ability like that. In my thirteen wins before then I had knocked out some opponents, but not the ones with big reputations. Bill Martin, assisting Jim ringside, cheered for my victory. My biggest fan of all, my wife, jumped into the ring with tears in her eyes. The largely Mexican crowd was silenced by my performance. I was now the North American Boxing Federation Champion (N.A.B.F). It was as though I was walking out a vision I had never seen before. I felt like a vessel, carrying out a movie script. I thanked God for the strength to accomplish my heart's desire. Now I would go down in the record books and would later defend the title a number of times against fighters like Sammy Stewart, Mike Trejo, and Miquel Grannados.

After defending the N.A.B.F. title three times I had an elimination bout to determine who should get the World title opportunity. I was up against a guy who was nicknamed "the Columbian Destroyer," Ilido Julio. He was undefeated at seventeen wins and no losses; all seventeen wins were by knockouts.

The fight took place on October 1st, 1997 at the Arrowhead Pond in Anaheim, California. It was an all out war, but what I remember particularly about this fight was the fact that Ilido was indeed the dirtiest opponent I had ever faced in the ring. From head butting to hitting behind the head and everything else he could get away with, he did. My corner men Angelo and Jim were great at keeping me focused on the task. It was a nasty fight because I had never faced such rage in all my years of fighting in the ring. "When the going gets tough, the tough gets going," would prove to be a true statement for me.

My wife watched the fight on television from the home we purchased three months earlier in O'Fallon, Illinois. Everyone except Lakiesha watched, because she had seen me box on countless occasions since being a toddler. She found comfort in knowing I could take care of myself pretty well inside that four squared circle. As the story goes, Lakiesha went to bed while the other two stayed up with their mom late into the night, cheering feverishly as I knocked out "the Destroyer" late in the eleventh round with a mean right hand. A hush fell over the mixed crowd of thousands; this was such a tough fight that the injuries I suffered would be felt for years.

Sometime later as I viewed the video of the fight, I spotted my opponent crying in his corner after getting up off the mat very wobbly. When the referee called a halt to the fight I thought, *You got what you deserved.* I still feel the same, for I believe the saying, "cheaters never win."

Now I was ranked the number one flyweight in the world.

A mandatory title challenge against the World Champion didn't come without a challenge from the adversary. I remember times that my spirit was attacked while winning and defending my N.A.B.F title. I woke up countless nights in my home or on the road in a very cold sweat and my weary soul found no rest. I had been taught by Clara as a young Christian that the name of Jesus alone made the enemies flee.

I understood my struggles and that my story would be told one day.

CHAPTER 15

TKO:

A Blessing in Disguise

I was ready to make my move again for the world title. Mark Johnson was the first ever to win the flyweight crown as an African American. Johnson won the champion belt from a Columbian fighter in Las Vegas. This takeover of the championship didn't need the help of the judges; Mark Johnson knocked out the Columbian in the first round. It was good to know that if a decision had to happen between me and him, perhaps it might be fair. The title had changed hands a couple of times since Pichit had to retire and with this particular title, the International Boxing Federation Champion comes the prestige that every boxer wants. The winner would be the true champion because the I.B.F was an American ran organization and it had an outstanding reputation.

The theme for this fight was called "the battle of the Johnsons" scheduled to take place February 23rd, 1997 in Washington D.C. The champion's promoter, Cedric Kushner, was basically solely responsible for the promotion of this match. Angelo had worked with Kushner previously, so he felt that we could get a fair shake out of this bout, especially if I legitimately beat Johnson.

As I prepared to challenge Johnson for the title, I began to have trouble maintaining my weight. At one point during the preparation I told Jim that I didn't believe that I could get down to the 112 pound flyweight division. My body just couldn't perform down at that level anymore. But he persuaded me to train a little harder with hopes that the weight would fall off. Looking back I really felt I had made that weight one too many times. My body had grown a bit since my Olympic days and since the fight I had against Pichit in Thailand. I pushed myself beyond the limits to win the North American title and to keep defending that title.

One day after training for the Mark Johnson fight, I decided I should call my manager Angelo and talk it over with him. I wanted to tell him that I didn't think I could make the weight anymore, but when I call his office in Florida, there was no one in the office to answer. I began to rethink my options; *did I really want to pull out of this scheduled event? and a shot at a world title?* I worked so hard to earn this chance and thinking it over in my mind I realized that I was going to do whatever it took to get down there and win this time. I wanted it so badly I could taste it.

I continued training, literally starving myself to get my weight down. Although I felt my trainer should have seen through my suffering, in the end no one was to blame more than me. I felt that if I could get my weight down, perhaps I could control it. I did all the necessary things I needed to do for the fight, but the weight drained me all the while. Angelo was unaware of my struggles until afterwards. As the date drew nearer I ate less and trained harder, making my body break down in ways it never had before.

The bout took place at the Washington D.C Armory and was televised live on ESPN, to be watched by million. This was one of the most highly anticipated fights of its time, for those who knew the sport of boxing. The press conference took place a month before the fight in Washington. I was accompanied by Bill Martin, who had become one of my strongest supporters as well as having an invested interest, although I can truly say that it was never about money with Bill. Just the fact that he wanted to see me succeed was well worth all the risk he took to sponsor me. Neither Jim nor Angelo could make it to the press conference, but a huge crowd had come to witness this historical event. As the champion and I shook hands, we gave our opinions of what we thought would happen in the fight a month later.

At the weigh in a month later another huge gathering appeared. I gave them something to see; never before had I been so flamboyant, but now I said to the crowd, "I am the true champion" and, directed to Mark, "give up the title easy or die trying to keep it!" This was years of built up frustration speaking loud and clear and I didn't care. I felt that it was time for justice to be served. As the home crowd raged and booed, a few argumentative words were spoken by Mark to his followers. Everyone in boxing knew I should have been the World Champion by now.

I weighed in a pound under the limit, at 111 pounds, and my supporters cheered. My trainer, manager, wife, family, and friends had come to see me. The champion weighed the limit of 112 pounds and his followers cheered for him. Twenty four hours later the stage would be set for my chance to get my World title. I knew that this was my time—everything pointed to this night. But there was one major problem: I had starved myself for so long that my blood sugar dropped unknowingly to a very low point. This made my low weight very easy to maintain, but the danger was that I was unaware of the terrible turn my body had taken because of the sugar level problems. I was unable to regain any weight back for fight time. Countless times before, I had been able to gain weight after the weigh in, but even the day of the fight I ate everything I could but only gained two to three pounds, when I should have gained seven to nine pounds.

The morning of the fight I called my wife's room at the hotel. I had one of the worst headaches I had ever experienced before a fight. She came to my room very quickly, I explained to her what was happening to me and the first thing we did was pray about it. It never dawned on us that I was very ill. Perhaps we both thought that the headache would pass, but it never did, even after taking a bite to eat it would only go away for awhile. I thought perhaps it was just an attack from the adversary against me, because I knew him as an old foe, but this was a situation I ignorantly brought on myself like so many fighters do. Some have been known to die from situations like this one. I never wanted to complain to my trainer and manager because I didn't want them being negative about the situation.

After taking my last meal I was still battling the off and on headaches. The limousines came to take us to the National Armory, where we would be checked by security before entering. This was definitely some sort of indication to me that we were in the the bad part of town. Never before had I experienced security at this level before fight. My supporters felt a bit uncomfortable as well. I made my way to the locker room and I could hear my opponent in the very next room saying, "I ain't ready to give up my title. I will keep it." As I began to dress for the fight, a feeling of weakness began to creep over me; the headache and the pains that I had felt earlier that morning came back. I became exhausted and weak only seven minutes before the fight.

Bill Martin noticed my strange posture but could not put it together that something was terribly wrong. Instead of seeing me warming up as usual, he saw me sitting down. But Angelo and Jim never noticed a thing. I just didn't want to complain. I should say that I think most athletes are like that. They would rather suffer than complain, even if it's a matter of life and death. I think the old saying, "A quitter never wins," steps over its boundaries in issues concerning an athlete's health and safety.

An ESPN affiliate informed my corner men Angelo, Jim, and Bill, that we were up next after the commercial break. For the next couple of minutes before the fight, I sat in a chair, trying to preserve what little energy I felt I had left. With about a minute to go I tried to move around a little by shadow boxing. It was now time for me to walk down to the ringside. Going down to the ring from my locker room seemed very spacey and as I made my way to the ring I thought that once the fight got going my adrenaline would kick in and get me through it. My thoughts became very cloudy as I waited for the champion to enter the ring after me.

The loud roar of the crowd told me Mark Johnson was on his way to the ring. He was mounted on a large straw chair, symbolizing his Kingship as the reigning champion. He approached the crowd of thousands roaring cheerfully in the arena and millions cheering via television. As the introductions took place it was quite obvious who the crowd was for. Interestingly, as an amateur I had faced the champion's brother on a couple of occasions and I lost controversially in both cases, so I was looking toward evening the score with Mark. Mark's father and trainer had been around for that and was well aware of my intentions.

After the introductions fans from around the world expected a hellacious battle between us. The famous ESPN announcer Al Bernstein had given a lot of input during the buildup of this fight about how he thought it would go down. Both fighters came to the center of the ring to get last minute instructions. I noticed Mark refused to look me in the eyes. Of course that didn't matter to me, I just happen to notice it.

The bell rang for round one and I came out moving around the ring, flicking jabs in his face, which seemed to bother him quite a bit. I went on auto pilot; though everything still seemed very slow to me because of my weak feelings inside. Mark threw a looping punch, which braised my chin area. I became mildly defensive as I danced over by the ropes and Boom! He landed a punch I never saw coming from his unorthodox southpaw stance. Because I had no resistance whatsoever, down I went and the headaches came back as I laid flat on my back. By the time the referee counted to seven, my warrior's heart attempted to get up, but the referee prevented me from doing so.

Just like that, it was over.

The referee called a halt to the action, one minute and forty two seconds into the first round.

The crowd went mad as Mark celebrated by stomping around the ring. He was surprised as well, which he explained to the television announcer Mr. Bernstein. I got to my feet after the referee stopped the fight; there was no argument that I had been hurt. I remember afterwards Mark came over and asked me if I was alright, which showed good sportsmanship on his part. I responded by saying yes, that I was alright.

When the interviews took place I explained that Mark was a great champion and that he landed a great shot. I never complained once about my illness, which contributed largely to the fight's outcome. I had never been knocked out by anyone in all my years of fighting. I had only been knocked down once by a Cuban boxer as an amateur, but I was able to get back up and actually beat him down for doing so. But in this case, there would be no getting up. I lost in my third attempt to become champion of the World.

As I climbed out of the ring I heard a youngster say, "Where in the hell is your God now?" for it was known publicly that I was a preacher. The shout echoed of the insult to my mother in my last major match. The hurt I felt was indescribable, but more, I knew what a sad, lost person the kid had to be to say something so terrible.

My supporters followed me back to the locker room. I remember my niece Yvette wrapping her arms around me saying, "I'm very proud of you. As far as I'm concerned, you've done great in your career and if you never want to fight again don't let anyone talk you into it." My friend Michael Cross said, "Arthur, he was very lucky. It was like rolling dice and he rolled a seven, but even if you were to fight him again, I would still pick you to beat him because I believe in you just that much. You're the greatest, man." With these comforting words I walked out of the arena with my head up.

Jim was hurt beyond what words could say. LaTanya noticed that his expression was one of shock. Millions of viewers watched from around the world as Al Bernstein broadcast, "This was not suppose to happen. This was not suppose to happen, but it did." Those words would ring for some time to come.

During the ride back to the hotel Angelo said, "Son, this has never happen to you before."

I nodded and he replied, "What the hell you gonna do?"

There is nothing you can say to something like that. It just knocked the wind right out of me. I became very withdrawn as supporters crowded my hotel room and I realized that they were all disappointed by the outcome of the match, too. One by one they began to clear the room. A friend of the family, Benny Lewis, said that even if I had asked him to leave he wasn't going to, because in my darkest hour he wanted to be there for me. Benny stayed for sometime until my wife came back to the room after having to step out for a brief moment. She arrived to see me sitting in the dark on a chair as Benny sat in one of the other chairs. The first words that came out of LaTanya's mouth were, "Oh no, we are not going to have a pity party."

As the night drew, I drifted off to bed unshowered and with my clothes on. My wife laid by my side and we could hear Mark and his crew celebrating the win outside of the hotel window. We just laid there and she began to pray these words: "Lord, my husband loves you and thanks you for having blessed him to come this far. But Lord, at this point he is so devastated and so God, I ask you to help him to leave this disappointing night here in Washington D.C. and ask that it travels no farther with him to our home."

That was the beginning of my healing.

LaTanya later explained to me that when I got hit by Mark and as I was falling down to the canvas she saw it as if my mother was laying me down carefully. Perhaps she was the angel that watched over me that night. I will never question what my wife saw, I can only say that I am thankful to have lived through it and able to write about it.

The next morning we said our goodbyes to those who drove to support me and we headed toward the airport to go home. It felt as though a death had occurred and that although I was surrounded by support, I was alone. I thought, *If only I could hold somebody's hand*, it could help shake this terrible feeling of being alone. My wife and other supporters all looked tired from the night before, so I put my head down and hoped the flight from Washington would be a quick one. That was the longest flight I can ever remember taking.

Even after we got home, I was still ill from having to make such a low weight. My heart fluttered uncontrollably. I saw my doctor within the days following to discover my blood sugar level was at an all time low and I was diagnosed with hypoglycemia. I also had to wear a heart monitor for a couple of days, because as it turned out it was discovered that I also had a multi-valve prolapse, which is common among most people living in the world. Being hypoglycemic explained the reason for my sickness in Washington D.C. My resistance level being as low as it was during fight time, my doctor later explained to me that it could have been fatal. If I had gone more rounds in the fight, I could have suffered some major blood clotting. What was looked at as a devastating loss was now a blessing in disguise.

I now understood the reason I was knocked out. Although no world class fighter wants to be knocked out for *any* reason, I could now accept it. Before I just couldn't get over the fact that something like that could have happened. I later explained my illness to my trainer and manager as well as the others who came to support me. Angelo, told me that if he had known, the fight wouldn't have happen. Certainly I learned that it was foolish for me to push myself to that extreme level. My wife vowed that it would never happen again. I had to put it all behind me and move forward now that I understood my illnesses. Because I was physically fit, my doctors felt that I could continue if that's what I desired to do. They didn't see anything life threatening, but it could be if I didn't take care of myself in the way I needed to. I had to believe that all things work together for the good of those who love the Lord and who are called to live out His purpose. I had to believe that even in this, God's purpose would prevail.

CHAPTER 16

Moving Forward:

Winning at Home

It was eleven months before I fought again, primarily because of the illness from the previous match. Despite the fact that I had been knocked out, many boxers were still afraid to compete against me. Without question I was certainly one of the most feared fighters in the world. I got my body back to normal after about a month or so and I began to train again. It was another one of those hard things to come back from. I just couldn't help asking God, "Why?" even though the answer to that question was obvious, I hated that it had to happen. Once and for all, I had to put that behind me and move forward.

Because it would be awhile before I would fight again, I began to explore my other talents like singing and writing songs. I always had a knack for those things while growing up in East St. Louis. One Sunday morning while attending a church service in Cahokia, Illinois I met a fellow by the name of Jon Paul Sousan, who was a music producer visiting from Poplar Bluff, Missouri. He performed a couple of songs from his music project during the service. I thought before hand to myself, *Where do you meet these producers?* I met Jon Paul after the service to spark a conversation. I told him I had been a musician for a long time and often thought about recording. I had a lot of time on my hands so I asked him if he would consider producing a music project for me.

I sent Jon Paul a tape of some songs I wrote and sang, a couple of days later and he was elated with my talent and agreed to produce my first contemporary Christian CD titled, "The Best Thing." Long before I decided to use Arthur Anthony as my musical stage name, I used what most people knew me by—"Flash Johnson." After all the hard work the project soared to the number one listened to CD over the internet. It was exciting to have had done something of this magnitude outside of my boxing career. I can truly say that if I hadn't lost to Mark Johnson, perhaps I wouldn't have seized the opportunity to pursue my music; it actually helped me to look at other things I enjoyed doing. It all worked together for my good and what's more, I found a very good friend in Jon Paul. I worked with him on the CD often and got to know his family well.

Even while making the album, I continued to train and work harder. I still found the time to record, but stayed determined that I would one day reach my goal of being champion of the world. In the midst of all the hard work, tensions began to flare between Jim and me. After all the years we had spent together, we had reached a point where we no longer saw eye to eye on certain issues concerning my career. I decided that it would benefit me most for us to go our separate ways. I felt that he no longer had the respect for me that he once did and because it's my career we were debating about, I wanted no regrets. I had learned that it had to be my way, not anybody else's.

I had trained with Jim since I began boxing as a kid. Now I had to try to hire another trainer to replace him. It would be difficult, but I trusted God to lead me and he did. Winston Shaw, in whose gym I once trained in St. Louis, would become my new trainer. After much thought I knew that Winston would be great because I was familiar with him and worked with him a little back in my early days of boxing. Everyone called him "Buddy," which I always thought made him seem like a friendly sort. I became comfortable with him being my trainer because we seemed to have the same philosophy and he understood the game better, I felt, because he had done it himself. His personal experience with boxing allowed him to be a little more in tune with me as a fighter.

Buddy and I decided that I would move up in weight so that the problems, which occurred in my last bout, would be far from me. And so I did, moving to the bantamweight division at 118 pounds. I got in touch with Angelo and his first words to me were, "Do you still want to go after the title?" My answer to him was, of course, "Yes!" There were times that I had considered retiring, but after my telephone conversation with Angelo, I was sure this was what I wanted to do: to continue moving forward.

A couple of months later I was on track to step into the ring once again against Reuben Contreaus of New Mexico. The fight was in my home area of St. Louis, Missouri, at the Regal Front Hotel Downtown. This was only my second time fighting near home in my career and this would be the closest as it would seem that I would ever come to competing across the river in East St. Louis. Even though I always wanted to compete at home, there were no promoters willing to take that chance.

After not being in the ring for eleven months I wondered how I might look in front of my home crowd who made their way over to support me in January of 1999. I remember a guy coming up to me before the bout to inform me that Leon Spinks heard that I was fighting and he wanted to show his support by being there. I felt honored that heavy weight champion Leon Spinks wanted to see me. He offered his hand, standing alongside of the gentleman who introduced him, and I graciously shook it. I knew there were a lot of people who showed up to cheer me on, but my friends and family members would be proud of me no matter what the outcome was. My record at this time was eighteen wins against four defeats and I wasn't looking forward to losing anymore.

During the night of my comeback, a terrible incident occurred involving a Mexican fighter named Ibarra. He fought just two bouts before me in an over-matched fight against a ranked Thailand fighter competing as a bantamweight. He suffered a blood vessel broken in the brain area as he was knocked out by the Thailand fighter. The damage was unknown as he made his way back to his locker room, right next to mine. A few moments later, he passed out and needed emergency attention in order to save his life.

With all of this going on it was hard to stay focused on the business in which I had to attend to. I whispered a prayer up for him as he was rushed to St. Louis University Hospital, not knowing what his condition was. His situation was unknown to the huge crowds that was in attendance. Meanwhile the show was not going to be cancelled (in most cases they never are), and what's worse, I was fighting against his stable mate, who I am sure was concerned about his friend.

The fight just before ours involved a kid I had fought in my seventh pro fight, just before my first title shot. His name was Arturo Estrada and the fight first ended with him declared the winner. Arturo's opponent could not continue because he was counted out after falling out of the ring. After further review it was decided that Arturo actually pushed his opponent and the verdict was changed. He was disqualified and the victory went to his opponent, Jason Pierz, who was the defending U.S.B.A. Featherweight champion. Arturo was also the stable mate of the kid that got hurt. After he found out about Ibarra he took it very hard. While Arturo was fighting, he had no idea what had happened after Ibarra walked back to the locker room.

After the drama of the previous two bouts, it was now time for what most people came to see. As I entered the ring the crowd roared, still unaware of the Ibarra incident just moments before. My opponent Reuben, was much closer to Ibarra than I was, so I know it had to be weighing heavily on his mind. The introductions were made and it seemed that Rueben knew he had come to the lion's den. For me, it was a good change being at home after much travel in other fighter's hometowns; it was good to have the "home field" advantage. Even though I fought in the last bout of the evening, I don't believe one soul left the site. My children saw me fight for the first time live and what a thrill it was for them.

As the fight started the crowd of thousands stood on their feet. Now my mind was able to focus on the match. I wasn't sure about my opponent's thinking, but I couldn't concern myself with that. It's a fighter's rule that only the business inside of the ring should concern him. I knew I had to be focused to perform well and it was with the first meaningful punch I threw to his body that ended the fight at one minute and thirty seconds in the first round.

The celebration started immediately after the fight, but my concern switched back to Ibarra as I wondered how he was and if he was going to make it. After a small celebration with my family and friends, I couldn't help but be occupied by the Ibarra situation. The very next morning my new friend Jon Paul and I went to the hospital where Ibarra was. It was tough getting in there because he had been left all alone until his family members could make it in to see him. Once the hospital administrators found out who I was, they agreed to let me see him. I made my way to his room as his first visitor; his trainer and manager left to go back to Mexico. I couldn't understand why no one stayed to be with him—he was young and in his prime at twenty one years of age. What I entered the room to witness was a horrible after-fight coma.

Lying all alone, it reminded me of an old incident involving a kid I once sparred with in the beginning of my comeback in Minneapolis. His name was Simon, and I found out he had been shot in the head at point blank range. He too lie in a coma and I went to visit him and his family there in the hospital. They wanted me to pray for him, as they had heard that I was a minister apart from being a fighter, so I laid my hands on him and prayed for him. God granted Simon a miracle. The next time I saw him he was working out in the gym some time later.

I wasn't sure that Simon's miracle would happen for Ibarra. I thought it was truly a shame that he was left in St. Louis, all alone. I felt it necessary to stay there and check on him from time to time, laying hands on him and praying for him until his family members got there. His was one of the most highly recognized incidents in the sport of boxing at that time. I was able to stay away from the media and I would spend hours with him until his first family member arrived. His mother came a couple of days later. It took time for her to get a visa and money, because as I found out later, they were incredibly poor and Ibarra had come to fight to make money for his family. He came to America to help his family in the only way he knew how.

That's the bad end of boxing because obviously his manager cared nothing about him. I had also heard that he wasn't as prepared as he should have been. Of course that's speculation, because you never know what will happen in a boxing ring. I wanted to stay with him because I felt that if it had been me, my wife would have wanted someone there to comfort me if she could not be there. I stayed by his side, praying for him to pull through. When his mother arrived she was gracious that I looked after him. Some days later his father was able to join his mother, but before he arrived I was able to get LaTanya to help comfort his mother. It was hard trying to communicate because I spoke no Spanish and she spoke no English, but the human spirit is remarkable in that she understood my concern for her son. At times we could find an interpreter to help us communicate with one another, and I talked with her and cried with her. I am sure that gave her the comfort that he wasn't alone. Bill, one of the guys who remained in my corner, gave her some added monies to help in her time of need. We did all we could to help make the situation more bearable.

As time went by I continued to check on the Ibarra family after my gym workouts, believing in God and praying for a miracle. Ibarra laid in a coma for a month and one day I walked in to visit him and he was sitting up! God gave him a miracle just as he did Simon, many years earlier. Even the doctors were confused in that they could not see how this young man pulled through. It was great to see God answer a heartfelt prayer in which makes man admit that they had nothing to do with it. One of the doctors gave a television interview to the local news, in which he said, "I was just the hands in the surgery, but God was the healer."

To this day the Ibarra family and I remained good friends. He would have to come back for a second surgery some time later, which consisted of a piece of bone being place back in his head because it had to be removed to release the swelling to his brain. His family contacted me to let me know that everything went great.

I continued to train throughout this situation and another door was open to me: an opportunity to win the National Boxing Association Bantamweight World title. The N.B.A. was the very first boxing organization that was ever established, which included champions like Henry Armstrong, Joe Louis and Sugar Ray Robinson. Just like that, another shot at a world title, an impressive fourth attempt, was given to me. Again, there are great fighters who never get one shot at a world title, and I must say for that I was thankful.

CHAPTER 17

Fourth Try

Fighting for the N.B.A. title was completely unexpected. Angelo Dundee mistakenly thought it was for the N.A.B.F., which was a title I had won earlier in a lighter weight class. Boxers and managers talk about boxing titles by abbreviation in most cases, which can get incredibly confusing as several sound alike. Matchmaker Payton Sher gave me the opportunity to fight earlier in St. Louis, and Angelo decided to continue to use him to get fights for me. Sher contacted Angelo about an opportunity involving promoter Dana Pitcher from Louisiana. This would be his first time promoting boxing and wanted me to fight for the title.

Suddenly I was fighting for a world title again. It happened so quickly that I didn't have a chance to focus on the question on everyone's mind: would I win it in my fourth attempt? I didn't even realize I was going to fight for a title other than the N.A.B.F. I arrived in Louisiana, tried to get relaxed, and went for a small, light workout. A couple of days away from the fight, I was sitting on my bed relaxing and I thought I would watch a little television before meeting with my trainer, Buddy. A television commercial came on, which stated I was to fight for the N.B.A. World Title. It was once again before me, a clear reality. I contacted Angelo in Miami, who couldn't make it out to the fight, but responded, "Win that title kid."

My opponent, Roberto Lopez, was from New Mexico. As fight time drew near we both weighed in at 117 pounds, one pound lighter than the 118 pound bantam weight limit. I was not able to sleep the night before the fight, but I trusted God would give me the strength to equal the task, which laid ahead of me. My wife, who had come to support me, came over to my hotel room to help me relax so that I could get some sleep.

On the following day my opponent and I came to challenge each other for the making of history. As was my custom, I studied tapes of my opponents during my preparation and this one was certainly no exception. I was confident that I could win, as every fighter who steps into the ring is. I always knew that the opportunity would come unexpectedly, but I had to be ready to seize the moment. I was prepared to overcome the challenges I was about to face. I had a short time frame to make it happen, but a lifetime to think about it and I only wanted great thoughts. As the night of the fight quickly came my supporters arrived, hoping that a long time desire would be fulfilled. I learned that my real friends stuck with me no matter what the outcome.

The time came to fight for the right to be called World Champion, a night in which I would remember for years to come. A flashback of what happened a year ago when I fought Mark Johnson, went through my mind. Could I withstand a big league punch as I had in the early stages of my career? The fight brought thousands of fans out to the Cajun Dome in Lafayette, Louisiana, a place that never held any event of this sort. They all came to witness this World Championship fight.

Roberto and I approached the ring, Roberto first then me. The crowd roared as the introductions were made. From the sound of the first bell it was quite evident that there were a large number of Mexican fans in attendance. But there was quite a number of African Americans as well. I could feel who was rooting for whom. The first round brought a challenge for me because Roberto landed some big time blows that I had to withstand. As the fight progressed I began to get stronger, despite the fact that Roberto had been at the bantamweight division a bit longer than I had. It didn't seem to make a difference in terms of strength as I started to wear him down with vicious shots to the body throughout rounds two and three. By the fourth round he dropped to one knee and was counted out.

The crowd absolutely exploded. I had finally done it after being denied three times before.

I was now Champion of the World of the National Boxing Association, the motherhood of all the titles in boxing.

It felt great as I mounted the ropes to the roar of the crowd after being announced as the new champion. What's even better is that the title was vacant, meaning it was just waiting for me as I saw it and I didn't have to challenge anyone else for it. My family and I celebrated the goal accomplished that night and again we celebrated when we got home to O'Fallon. I have learned any great accomplishment that goes unrecognized goes uncelebrated. Immediately after the fight I called my friend Michael Cross who could not make it. To hear him rejoice with me was wonderful. It was an awesome night to remember and it was good to know my opponent had no permanent injury, just the shame of being defeated by T.K.O.

I have got to tell you I was blessed to achieve something that many fighters have desired but never reached. I believe with all my heart that the purpose of God was accomplished in my boxing career. I know he wants me to have it all, but I believe that he is more concerned with the character of a man than the man's desires. Certainly through my trials and triumphs my character was indeed formed.

Often times my mind flashed back to the very beginning. I had hoped for great things, but I never knew for sure it would be all that I had hoped for. From my first experience with boxing in East St. Louis, to my reign as champion of the World, God used boxing to help me prosper greatly. Boxing brought me from the projects and poverty, and it opened doors for me to pursue my music and to have a prosperous family.

God says in his word that your gift will make room for you and bring you before great men. I am honored to have been before them all, from the United States President to the Russian President, Prime Ministers, Ambassadors, Governors, Senators, and a load of others. I met celebrities and the likes, some of which I was glad I met, and some in which I was sorry I met, but it showed me the sort of person I wanted to be and I've learned that we're all just humans subject to failure.

As I look back I don't hold any grudges against those who caused me hardship, even though forgiveness took a long time. I thank God for the experience that I have had so that I may help others who travel down that same road I once struggled down. There were lessons learned that will never be forgotten. I've often prayed that ignorance of this sort travels no further as it relates to manmade religion, which is bondage. God says, "My people perish for lack of knowledge"; hopefully my story will better help you to understand the tricks of the adversary. God is very direct and not a bunch of do's and don'ts. Learn to seek God for yourself very early in your Christian walk because even being a babe in Christ, God is able to meet you on whatever level you may be on. God won't allow you to go astray and he will give you a pastor after his own heart.

CHAPTER 18

Life After Boxing

A year after retiring from the ring, I began to settle down a bit and think about what I wanted to do. Without question, I wanted to continue to pursue my music, but outside of that I got the idea to write an autobiography about my life as a boxer. I thought that because of how my career came to be and the trials I suffered to achieve my dreams; it could make for an interesting story.

Meanwhile I felt I needed to get into the swing of a normal life, which meant I would have to find a job. Unfortunately the last couple of fights I had that were promoted by my own company didn't fare so well—in fact, we lost a gang of money on them. Because of this, I realized it was time to move on. I took a job as a security officer for a little while to establish myself as an employee.

Just as I began to adjust to my new career, I received a disturbing phone call from my sister, Theresa. She told me that my younger sister, Regina, was in a car accident with her family and she was the only one who did not survive. I remember that I was in the middle of cutting my hair as I answered this phone call and I tried to make sense out of Theresa, who was crying and talking at the same time. As she told me that Regina died in a terrible car accident, I dropped the phone and my heart began to beat harder than ever before and tears rolled down my face. I had never been so shocked and so hurt at the same time; I didn't know what to do. The fact that they were still living in Minnesota and I was living with my own family in Illinois made it that much more difficult to bear.

As my family gathered for this great sad occasion, it was the hardest thing we had faced as siblings. I thought if it was possible to die from a broken heart, that I would. I had never witnessed my wife so broken as she was in that moment because she and my sister were very close. Life just would not be the same without Regina. I cried for a very long time, even after the funeral. One thing I can say is that she wouldn't have wanted anyone else in her family to have died in that accident. Regina's husband had a rough time moving on with their four children, but God graced him with the courage to do so and of course our family came together to support him and the children during this most difficult time in their lives.

After the funeral, I returned to work as a security guard, but I started to think about returning to the ring again. It was only two years after my last fight; it was in my blood to want one more title, but in truth, one more would always lead to one more. I called my former manager, Angelo, to talk about my return to the ring and he said, "Great!" I started to train, but my body began to take a different turn than it had before. Even so, I was very quickly placed in the top ten ratings for a championship fight, despite my two years off. I was still regarded as a world-class fighter until it was proven otherwise. But before that fight could happen, a tougher fight would intervene.

During my training I noticed I wasn't feeling normal, so I went to my doctor. He performed a routine checkup and ordered everything from blood work to x-rays to find out what was different about my body. The x-rays discovered a large mass on my intestines, which my doctor thought could only be cancer.

Before beginning a rigorous treatment, I was scheduled for an appointment at the hospital to make sure of what we would be dealing with. Before this procedure would take place I asked a couple of friends to come to my home for a prayer session. My friends and family placed their hands on me and prayed for my recovery. At that moment, I felt a warm sensation go through my body and I just knew that whatever the doctors found on that x-ray would be gone.

My doctor was already talking about chemotherapy, because everything pointed towards cancer at this time. The procedure I was to have at the hospital meant an end to my boxing career; I would not be able to come back from the incision they needed to make in my abdomen. I made my peace with that and continued on with the operation. As the doctors combed through my intestines to confirm the diagnosis of the x-rays, they found absolutely nothing—in fact my intestines were as clean as a newborn's.

After a remarkable recovery from such an invasive surgery, I landed my dream job. I became a vocational school spokesman, with the aim of reaching out to people to go to college. I loved working in this capacity and I felt it helped my healing process. Unfortunately this company didn't last very long, but I found my new calling in working with children who had learning disabilities. These children were a part of a behavioral management programs in Illinois that provided support for children with learning disabilities that didn't allow them to function in a regular school. This job was very beneficial in teaching me a lot about patience and gave me a sense of helping others.

It took awhile for me to heal and to accept that my boxing career was completely over.

CHAPTER 19

The Greatest Comeback

A few years later I found myself in a set place at a set time for what was about to become the biggest fight of my life since existing on this earth. I was up against what is perhaps the greatest affliction a human being can ever be stricken with.

It started one morning when I went for a jog with my son and his friend. I noticed that I had no kick in the end of our six mile run and afterwards it took quite a while before I could quit gasping for air. I realized that my body couldn't relax and get back to a restful state after that long run. After showering my wife noticed my slumped posture and a day or so later she noticed bruises on the backs of my legs, which brought her great concern. I thought they would soon go away, that perhaps I bruised myself while running. I was attending summer classes that I thought would be beneficial to my own business and during one of the class periods I happened to look down and notice disturbing bruises on my knees. I thought it was incredibly strange, but I was still physically feeling fine. The next morning I was at a summer program where I worked with young students who had learning disabilities. During my lunch break I noticed a lump on my arm and thought, *Is this a blood clot?* Another staff member noticed my concern and stated, "Call your doctor. If you don't, I will." It was his comment that inspired me to see my doctor, since this was the third or fourth strange thing I'd noticed happening to my body.

My doctor checked me over and said, "Arthur, I have no idea what that lump could be," so he ordered blood work that Friday. On Sunday I was the opening act for a performance by the legendary group, The Delphonics. By the time I had to perform I was starting to deteriorate quickly. I began to notice blood in my urine, but still I persevered. After getting home from a great performance, my condition continued to worsen. My urine was now an indescribable color, my stool had blood in it, and I was beginning to display flu-like symptoms. I told my wife about the changes and she called our oldest daughter, Lakiesha, who was studying medicine at the time in Chicago. Lakiesha informed her mother that she needed to get me to a hospital for fear that my kidneys were failing.

Before the blood tests from Friday could be documented, I was diagnosed with a rare form of Leukemia. Life as I knew it would never be the same.

From Sunday evening until Tuesday evening, Memorial Hospital in Belleville, Illinois fought to save my life. It happened so fast that I didn't understand how I got there and what went wrong so quickly. My wife and I were overwhelmed; we cried a million tears before anger set in. I had been diagnosed with Acute Promyelocytic Leukemia, a cancer of the blood and bone marrow that annually affects 1,500 people in the United States and only 3,500 people internationally.

Memorial Hospital did everything they could, but they just weren't equipped to handle such a rare and quickly spreading disease. I was transferred to the Siteman Cancer Center at Barnes-Jewish Hospital in St. Louis, Missouri by ambulance on Tuesday evening. I waited to go into a surgery, which would allow for medicine to be distributed throughout my veins to save my life. While waiting in the hallway of Siteman, I heard an evil force speak to my mind. It said, "I want your life." It was then that I said to God, "My time is in your hands." I found myself looking at a sudden end as my family and friends gathered in the waiting room.

Entering this procedure my doctor at Siteman said to me, "We must treat you very aggressively. If we do not, this will consume you within two to three months." The doctor fought to insert the medicine into my veins, but everything he tried, failed. Every vein in my arms had collapsed, so he needed to move the insertion to my lower extremities. It was too risky to chance creating an entry point in my neck, since I was in such bad shape at that point. The procedure was supposed to take 45 minutes, but it lasted hours. I was awake throughout the operation and I could hear the doctor becoming flustered. "I've done this many times, but today, it's giving me serious problems," he said as I lay on the table. Again, I whispered to God, "My time is in your hands."

Finally, after bringing in a scope, he was able to make a connection to a major vein. The problem with this was that my veins were very close to the main artery, which made it risky and difficult. All I could think was, *All I want is a chance. God, just give me a chance.* Now I had a chance to survive. I knew that if given a chance, the result would be favorable.

I was released from the hospital one month and one week later, making remarkable improvements. That was the closest to death that I had ever been.

La Tanya lived at the hospital with me, spending nights on the weekends. My children poured out an overwhelming amount of support. In fact Areda was there throughout the duration of my stay at the hospital, spending countless hours by my side. The day Areda was to return to college was the day I was given my discharge papers. I felt so blessed to have this kind of support from my entire family.

So many things happened during this time of my life that it was really too much to try to take in. But through it all, God was faithful. Like a fighter, if given the opportunity after being knocked down, he can get up and win. All I wanted was an opportunity, and He gave it to me.

For the next six months, chemotherapy was essential. I prayed over every dose administered to my body, prayed that it would accomplish its mission. The treatment involved in this stage was a drug called Arsenic. This is the chemical that kills rats. A doctor from Europe discovered that this treatment worked against the sort of cancer I was diagnosed with. It is still amazing to me that I wound up at this exact time and place—20 years earlier there wouldn't have been any hope for my survival.

During my treatments I experienced unforgettable things, like meeting people who eventually died. I recall meeting a young man by the name of Bennett, who was diagnosed with pancreatic cancer. I told him my name and he remembered hearing that I was a boxing champion. I prayed with him and I watched him fight to the very end. One day, while coming in for my treatment, I saw the familiar Spirit of Death upon him. It wasn't long before I didn't see Bennett anymore and I learned that he passed away. I watched countless others lose their fights while I kept returning for treatment.

If there is anything that I've learned from this experience, it is that there are no guarantees in life. During my fight, I thought about my mother, a lady who showed me how to deal with adversity. I wondered how she would have handled things and realized that I should model her behavior. So I comforted those who loved me, telling them that they would not lose me. I believe it helped because they could tell from the sound of my voice that I was confident in my convictions that I would survive this.

The weakness that overshadowed my body for one and a half years was finally defeated. Everything that could have gone wrong, did, for awhile as I fought off infections to my body. Through it all, I refused to let negative thoughts control how I felt about my body's progress. I wish I could say that it was easy, but I don't have that testimony. However, my faith is now stronger than ever. I believe the mind is the most important battle ground.

I often hear people say I was lucky, or I lucked out. Everyone who has ever fought this kind of disease has a different story, but for me, my experience is one of faith. And that's how I choose to live my life—by faith from Trials to Triumph.

CHAPTER 20

Ingredients for Success

"Greatness in whatever field you desire will come with a price."

The four things that I learned that are essential for greatness are Perseverance, Accuracy, Focus, and Timing. Perseverance must be displayed throughout, and dedication to achieve greatness no matter what. The mind must be willing and set, no matter the setbacks, delays, or hopelessness you will experience. You must keep moving forward. Those who watch can only be inspired. Accuracy is something that must be perfected with hard work, for I feel that good luck is the residue of very hard work. Repetition allows accuracy to flow like clockwork. Focus is inevitable regardless of what is happening around or to you. You must be and stay focused and remember, you must see it before anybody else sees it. Your response in crisis situations prepares you for greatness. And last but certainly not least is Timing. It is not when everyone around you recognizes the moment, and maybe perhaps not even you will feel that it is time. But when the doors open, timing will always come unexpectedly and the great ones know how to seize the moment. There is a time for everything under heaven to take place, but we must be ready.

Greatness is not a gift from God but an earned attribute. Another essential element to greatness is hope, which leads to belief. For without belief in God and yourself, you can withdraw your plea for greatness. Just as important as the other four, belief will carry you over and beyond. Greatness must simply start with one step of hope.

John says, "I wish above all things that you prosper and be in good health." I've learned that whatever your talent is, always recognize the strength given to you and give it all you've got. You may find yourself with a million excuses of why you should give up, but not one good reason. In the end you're the only one to blame because you're the only one who can defeat your destiny.

I believe that we are responsible for the talents God gives us and that we will have to give an account for what we've done with them in the end.

The parable of the talents in Matthew, Chapter twenty five, may help us to remember that the one who did nothing with his talent had it taken away from him. As for me, boxing was one of those earned talents. I was blessed to have the ability to learn, in that I was not the most gifted kid starting off. As a matter of fact I was one of the least gifted ones out of the bunch from the very beginning, but I had the potential to make something of myself and for that I am thankful to God for the ability and athleticism he gave to me. But earning my talent in boxing came with a dear price called strong will. That's something you have to develop yourself.

Whatever you accomplish in this life you will earn it, but just because you will earn it, recognize the giver of your strength by being humble. If you have to ask someone if you are humble, chances are you're not, but out of the same breath I must say as far as accomplishing your goals in life, no matter what they are, how you see yourself is how others will see you too.

Boxing was one of the hardest things I've ever experienced in my life, outside of having to overcome the most difficult battle of my life, which was against cancer. My situation was as unorthodox as they come. Nobody ever knew my struggles. Only my wife La Tanya and my dear friend Clara Johnson could make some sense of my experiences. During the fight for my own sanity, at times I felt all alone, but through it all I would have to ask myself if I knew what awaited me in my quest, would I do it again? Having gone through it, I would do it all again because I discovered if God is with me, I believe all things are possible.

CHAPTER 21

Finding Out Where You Belong

I believe I've been blessed to help shed the light on individuals who may be stuck in situations similar to mine. I want to help free you right now by saying that anytime your trust is in man rather than God, regardless of what man's position may be in life, you must remember that developing your own understanding of God is paramount to anyone else's interpretations.

Regarding religion, maybe it's nothing but a cult. When you feel you need someone's approval more than God's, that's one of the initial signs of a cult religion. It is vital that you understand that God hears your prayers, so allow yourself to be guided by Him and Him alone. I am not saying you won't experience some discomfort—because you most definitely will—but remember all things work together for the good of those who love Him. Those who are the called live according to His purpose and not anyone else's.

Whatever you have a desire to do most in life, that's indeed what you should be doing. It's all a part of the struggle in which we gain knowledge and experience and whatever we accomplish it is most appreciated when a struggle has been involved. Then and only then, you have a story to tell. When you find out where you belong and what you should be doing you'll become a strong force to be reckoned with, but first you must be convinced. Remember what the Apostle Paul said, "Let every man be persuaded by his own opinion and not by someone else's." You'll discover that life is good and you are meant to have journeys and experiences.

I remember reading about a person who said, "When my life is over, I want to have been spent entirely doing whatever good my hands found to do." Remember the words of your own mouth are powerful; you will have whatever you say you will because ordinary people achieve great things.

I look at myself and all the achievements I had in boxing. I kept moving despite the hardship and I discovered that faith is when, despite all obstacles, your hands and feet keep moving. So if ever you are challenged, let these very words ring in your ears: "I must keep moving."

See yourself in that place where you hope and want to be, for if you never see it, I promise you, you'll never be it. God says, "my people perish for lack of vision." Despite whatever kind of a long shot it may appear to be, see it and you'll began to see more than you ever thought you would.

"If when you tell others your dreams and goals and they don't laugh at them, chances are your dreams and goals aren't quite big enough." Every step of the way was I fought by the adversary for those who dare to be great must be up for the fight, and there will always be a fight. "The wealth of the world will never open up her mouth easily." But God spoke through John when he said, "I wish above all things that thou would prosper." You should also know that the same affliction that abides in you also abides in your brothers that are in the world. Though I have many friends that are not Christians, they have been affected by the integrity I maintained throughout my career.

I went further than I ever thought I would, winning two more world titles as a Junior Featherweight in my hometown of East St. Louis, a place in which I never thought I would fight as a professional, but I did after taking ownership of my career. Nothing ever compared to the night I won my first championship of the world. That night was such a reminder of the scriptures, when God says, "Exceedingly and abundantly above what you can even ask or imagine." One whispered prayer was answered in which I had asked God to bless me to become a world champion. I believe he helped me in the most unorthodox way by giving me the strength and allowing me to develop the will power to never give up.

In whatever you do, never give up, no matter how long the wait may seem. What you hope to receive someday is all in the wait. I suppose one of the hardest things I had to get over was something that I call "churchology," in other words worrying about how other Christians viewed my career or the fact that "churchology" is nothing more than a form of godliness. As I stated in time past. religion is demonic because it leaves the door open for other problems to escalate. I've discovered that if you are afraid to disagree or to confront life, you'll never be successful, because part of succeeding will lead to disagreements. If your aim in life is to please others in your decision making, you will most definitely be miserable, and what is life if it is lived being miserable? It's no life at all.

There are decisions in life we all have to make and live by. Sometimes on a day to day basis the choices you make determine where you live tomorrow. I believe we've all been given something good from God and what you do with that gift is your gift to God. I was given the ability to fight, among other gifts and talents. I once heard a person say learn what your name means it could play a significant role in your future; in fact the name "Arthur" means "warrior, King."

I hope you have been encouraged by my story. So now go and make your own story worth reading and remember, it all began with just one step. Best wishes.

ACKNOWLEDGEMENTS

First, I would like to thank God for having a story to tell. I hope that those who read my story can find encouragement in that one can overcome the odds no matter how dim they may seem.

I want to thank my wife, LaTanya, for her undying support and encouragement, as well as my daughters, Lakeisha and Areda, and my son, Arthur Jr.

I would like to express gratitude to those who had a hand in my success as an athlete: my former trainers and coaches, James Hooks, Benjamin Stiff, Frank Boarders, Theodore Myles, James Oldenburg, Kenny Loehr, Winston Shaw, and Angelo Dundee and my sponsors and friends Bill Martin and Michael Cross.

I would also like to mention the support of my surviving siblings, James, Theresa, Floyd, Albert, Stella, Pearlina, Ladonna, Maurice, and Calvin, my father, Arthur Allen, my stepmother Maggie, and my mother-in-law and family, Retha Harley.

My appreciation goes out to my publicist Dan Crain and editor Jayme Blandford.

Finally, I would like to dedicate this story to those who did not live to see this day and who I believe would have enjoyed the moment: my mother Estella, my sister Regina, and my godmother Clara Johnson.

In addition, to all other family, friends, and supporters, God Bless.

Other Projects Completed by the Author

Autobiographical film
The Greatest Comeback
Produced by I.C.O.N.

Musical Albums
The Best Thing
Greatest Moments
Greatest Moments Faze 2

For more information or to book Arthur for speaking
engagements, please visit: www.ArthurAnthony.org

To learn more about the
Arthur Johnson Foundation write
P.O. Box 882
O'Fallon Illinois
62269

CPSIA information can be obtained at www.ICGtesting.com
Printed in the USA
LVOW01s0205180814

399544LV00002B/6/P